THE LOGIC OF
PASSION

THE LOGIC OF PASSION

THE LITERARY CRITICISM OF WILLIAM HAZLITT

JOHN L. MAHONEY

New York
FORDHAM UNIVERSITY PRESS
1981

© Copyright 1978 by John L. Mahoney
© Copyright 1981 by FORDHAM UNIVERSITY PRESS
All rights reserved
LC 81-67501
ISBN 0-8232-1073-1 *(clothbound)*
ISBN 0-8232-1074-X *(paperback)*
Preliminary edition 1978
Revised edition 1981

To
JOHN, PAT, and BILL,
my continuing sources
of
inspiration

All quotations of Hazlitt's writings are taken from *The Complete Works of William Hazlitt*, ed. P. P. Howe, 21 vols. (London: Dent, 1930–1934).

Contents

Preface	ix
Introduction	1
1 The Critical Setting	7
2 Intellectual Forebears	27
3 A New Image of the Critic	37
4 Art and the Living Reality of Nature	45
5 Gusto and the Reasons of the Heart	61
6 The Higher Law: Disinterestedness, Sympathy, Objectivity	73
7 Imagination and the Ways of Genius	87
8 Literature, Criticism, and the New Manifesto	101
Bibliography	115
Index	121

Preface to the Revised Edition

IT IS SOME THREE YEARS since *The Logic of Passion* first saw the light. A preliminary edition was published under the aegis of the Institut für Englische Sprache und Literatur of the University of Salzburg, whose Salzburg Studies in English Literature, under the direction of Professor Edwin A. Stürzl, has brought forth a distinguished list of important works in English studies. One important phase of their venture has been the Romantic Reassessment series, under the vigorous and supportive editorship of James Hogg, in which the present work was originally No. 75. Although the edition was limited to 250 copies, printed offset from typescript and paperbound, it won such gratifyingly favorable reviews that I was emboldened to look for publication under American academic auspices. This edition is the result of that search, and it incorporates a number of necessary, if essentially minor, modifications to what is substantially the work which first appeared in 1978. The only negative note in all the reviews known to me was one critic's regretting the absence of an index; this has now been provided. For Dr. Hogg's ceding of the earlier publication rights and for Fordham University Press's preparation of this new edition, I am deeply grateful.

I should like to offer thanks, as well, to the many people who encouraged and assisted me in the preparation of this book.

Boston College has provided me with generous support for this venture, and with many of the practical necessities which an author needs in the preparation of a manuscript. Rev. Charles Donovan, s.j., University Historian, Rev. J. A. Panuska, s.j., Dean of Faculties, and Professor Donald

PREFACE

J. White, Dean of the Graduate School of Arts and Sciences, are humane and generous administrators who have never failed to show their interest.

Professor P. Albert Duhamel, my former teacher and present colleague, read the entire manuscript and made wise and constructive observations. My colleagues Paul Doherty, Joseph Longo, John McCarthy, Dennis Taylor, Andrew Von Hendy, and Alan Weinblatt have on many occasions listened to my ideas and given me the benefit of their criticism; the late Edward Hirsh shaped much of my thinking about eighteenth-century English literature.

Professor W. P. Albrecht of the University of Kansas has always stood for the best in Hazlitt scholarship and has been a model for me; he has always been ready to share his ideas. And any student of Hazlitt must feel indebted to the continuing concern of Professor James Houck of Youngstown University.

David Anderson, my former student, now Assistant Professor of English at Texas A & M University, corrected my faulty prose; and Marsha Ludwig did her usual expert job of typing. Patricia A. Mahoney advised me on matters of arrangement, and was of special help in the preparation of the typescript. The staffs of Boston College Library, Tufts University Library, and the Cary Memorial Library of Lexington, Massachusetts, provided invaluable assistance.

On a personal note, I offer special thanks to the memory of Teddi King, Irene Kral, and Josh Gerber. My gratitude also goes to Jackie and Roy Kral. All provided the precious gift of friendship and good music.

As always, my wife, Ann, has been my wise and firm adviser and my constant support.

Boston College
May 1981

Introduction

THE LIFE AND WORK of William Hazlitt have claimed the attention of biographers and critics from the period shortly after his death in 1830. The earliest attempts tended to be either too general or too eulogistic. Essays by E. L. Bulwer, Alexander Ireland, and George Saintsbury are examples of early and too enthusiastic appraisals; treatments like those of Leslie Stephen, Augustine Birrell, Percy Van Dyke Shelly, H. W. Garrod, and Jacob Zeitlin are of the general, appreciative variety.[1] P. P. Howe's *Life of William Hazlitt* (1922) is perhaps the real beginning of the modern phase of Hazlitt studies. The blustery and flamboyant critic and essayist, who typified in so many ways the dissent, the restlessness, and the idealism of English and European Romanticism, has since that time been the subject of a large number of studies. Howe, whose Centenary Edition of the works still stands as the most authoritative text, provided in his biography a precise and illuminating record of an exciting life which stood in marked contrast to so many earlier impressionistic and eulogistic treatments. His dispassionate and analytic approach is notably superior to the highly popular work of the prolific Hesketh Pearson whose *The Fool of Love* (1934) focuses to an almost inordinate extent on Hazlitt's celebrated love affair with Sarah Walker. Another biography, Catherine Maclean's *Born Under Saturn* (1943), reveals a special concern with Hazlitt's lifelong association with the tradition of Nonconformity and his persistent dedication to the cause of political and religious freedom. It remained, however, for Herschel Baker, in his *William Hazlitt* (1962), to provide what more than one reviewer has described as a magisterial study, the most thorough and searching general view of the man and his many facets. Baker's treatment of his life and its many associations with politics, religion, philosophy, and criticism has put all students of Hazlitt in his debt.

All the biographers point, of course, to Hazlitt's career as a literary critic, although only Baker provides any really extensive commentary on this dimension. In a relatively short but perceptive chapter on "The Making of the Critic," he traces Hazlitt's development as a critic, his associations with the journals of his age, the roots of his critical stance, and the general positions taken in his practical criticism. The chapter is a superb overview of the critic, although Baker suggests that critical theory is but a part of his venture and that a fuller and more comprehensive study of this large area is needed.

It is my concern with the specific question of Hazlitt's critical theory and practice which has occasioned this book. Again, critics have never been lacking for the task of providing some assessment of either the aesthetics or the criticism, although seldom has there been any large-scale attempt to see relationships between the two. Indeed, several scholars have provided the kind of foundation without which no student of Hazlitt can proceed. Elizabeth Schneider, for example, has detailed with extraordinary thoroughness the course of Hazlitt's intellectual development, especially as it relates to the parallel development of an aesthetic theory.[2] Her record of his reading and of the books which helped to shape a point of view is invaluable for anyone who would see the man in something more than an intellectual vacuum. At the same time she understandably pays less attention to the total critical output and to the specific demonstration of strong links between theory and practice in Hazlitt's varied critical investigations. The pioneering studies of John Bullitt and Walter Jackson Bate on the origin and growth of such key Hazlitt and Romantic themes as sympathy, wit, and imagination shed much new light on the criticism of the period, although their basic direction was theoretical.[3] The influence of these studies can be seen especially in Bate's short but seminal essay on Hazlitt in his *Criticism: The Major Texts* (1952), an essay which more than any other single work has contributed to an appreciation of Hazlitt as a major English critic and to a shattering of the traditional picture of him as a highly enthusiastic and impressionistic reviewer with little of value to say about literature and literary theory. It can also be seen in much of W. P. Albrecht's work, especially his *Hazlitt and the Creative Imagination* (1965), a book rich in contributions to an understanding of the development of a theory of creativity in Hazlitt but less interested in the enormous bulk of the critic's writings on literature. Roy Park's *Hazlitt and the Spirit of the Age* (1971) is an extremely valuable study of Hazlitt's aesthetic theory and of its philosophic roots in the eighteenth century, although Park quite validly pays less attention to the practical application of that theory. The studies by J. D. O'Hara and J.-C. Sallé of Hazlitt's ideas on imagination and association have also represented important advances in our understanding of the theoretical framework of the criticism without being directed to any great extent toward particular documents of criticism.[4] John Kinnaird, in his *William Hazlitt: Critic of Power* (1978), both keenly aware of and appreciative of the work of those who have gone before him, uses the concept of power as a way of getting at Hazlitt's perspective not only on literature but on politics, religion, manners, and morals. His is indeed a major study indispensable for anyone who would come to terms with the richness of Hazlitt's genius. Similarly, *The Letters of William Hazlitt* (1978), edited by Herschel Moreland Sikes, Willard Hallam Bonner, and Gerald Lahey, has provided a wealth of material on all aspects of Hazlitt's life and work.

Over the last forty years a number of shorter studies have focused on Hazlitt as a critic of specific genres and have limited themselves to his treatment of forms like poetry and the novel. Stanley Chase's "Hazlitt as a Critic of Art"; Charles Patterson's study of Hazlitt's treatments of prose fiction; Alvin Whitley's "Hazlitt and the Theater"; Albrecht's study of the criticism of tragedy; J. D. O'Hara's work on Hazlitt's theory of painting—these and several others are cases in point.[5]

The real need, in view of these approaches, is for a study which will look at the entire critical output, uneven and erratic though it be, to let it speak for itself first, and then to search out underlying forces and themes which give shape and direction to the work. This is what I have tried to do in the following chapters, attempting to go beyond the familiar and too often quoted sections of the criticism and to examine a wide variety of views and an equally wide variety of subjects. I have also tried to pose some basic questions about the relationship of an aesthetic to a body of practical criticism, a relationship which has not as yet, I think, been adequately explored. My hope is that something like a thorough introductory study of the criticism will emerge and that Hazlitt will be seen neither as the anti-intellectual critic dedicated to mere impressionism nor as an idealized literary connoisseur setting down elegantly framed rules for judgment. Certainly Hazlitt would recognize neither of these images since he so often saw himself as a harried, busy critic interested in large questions of artistic purpose, the nature of creativity, and the relationship of art to life, but also forced by circumstances beyond his control to make quick and hurried judgments about an incredible variety of literary and artistic problems.

The method of this book is thematic, my feeling being that chronological and modal approaches to Hazlitt's criticism, while having the advantages of neatness and clarity, frequently miss the rich variety and wide range of implication in that criticism. Chronological development is not a really vital factor in any view of Hazlitt as a critic; his positions remain fairly firm from the time he begins his career as a reviewer until the writing of his major statements. Treatments of Hazlitt solely in terms of his approach to particular genres or to other arts tend to distort the realities of

INTRODUCTION

his general approach, his tendency to use one genre to exemplify another, to make use of the interrelationships of the fine arts, to develop a dominant theme by exemplifying it in a variety of literary or artistic forms. Hazlitt is above all else a critic of strong feelings and sympathies, anxious to communicate the immediacy of his encounter with a work of art and to justify that encounter as a valid basis for judgment.

The opening sections of the book will briefly sketch the important questions of the setting of Hazlitt's criticism and the elements which seem crucial in the shaping of the critic's attitudes and viewpoints. It will then proceed in a series of chapters to consider what seem to be the major themes which run through the writings: the themes of nature, of emotional immediacy, of imagination, and of the end of literature and criticism. It should be said at this point that although this study will on many occasions deal with painting, sculpture, and music, the primary focus is literature and literary criticism, and that discussions of other arts are included only to illustrate or strengthen a pervasive issue or theme in Hazlitt's work.

NOTES

1. See *Literary Remains of the Late William Hazlitt with a Notice of His Life By His Son and Thoughts on His Genius and Writings*, edd. E. L. Bulwer and Sergeant Talfourd, 2 vols. (London: Saunders & Otley, 1836); Alexander Ireland, *William Hazlitt: Essayist and Critic* (London & New York: Warne, 1889); George Saintsbury, "Hazlitt," *Essays in English Literature* (London: Rivington, Percival, 1890), pp. 135–69; Sir Leslie Stephen, "William Hazlitt," *Hours in a Library*, 4 vols. (New York &

London: Putnam, 1904; repr. Grosse Point, Mich.: Scholarly Press, 1968), II 235–86; Augustine Birrell, *William Hazlitt*, English Men of Letters (London: Macmillan, 1926); *Essays by William Hazlitt*, ed. Percy Van Dyke Shelly (New York & Chicago: Scribner's, 1924); H. W. Garrod, "The Place of Hazlitt in English Criticism," *The Profession of Poetry and Other Lectures* (Oxford: Clarendon, 1929), pp. 92–109; Jacob Zeitlin, *Hazlitt on English Literature: An Introduction to the Appreciation of Literature* (New York: Oxford University Press, 1913).

2. *The Aesthetics of William Hazlitt: A Study of the Philosophical Basis of His Criticism* (Philadelphia: University of Pennsylvania Press, 1933).

3. John M. Bullitt, "Hazlitt and the Romantic Conception of the Imagination," *Philological Quarterly*, 24, No. 4 (October 1945), 343–61; W. J. Bate, "The Sympathetic Imagination in Eighteenth-Century English Criticism," *ELH*, 12 (1945), 144–64.

4. J. D. O'Hara, "Hazlitt and the Functions of the Imagination," *PMLA*, 81 (1956), 552–62; J.-C. Sallé, "Hazlitt the Associationist," *Review of English Studies*, N.S. 15 (1964), 38–51.

5. Stanley P. Chase, "Hazlitt as a Critic of Art," *PMLA*, 39 (1924), 179–202; Charles I. Patterson, "William Hazlitt as a Critic of Prose Fiction," ibid., 68 (1953), 1001–16; Alvin Whitley, "Hazlitt and the Theater," *The University of Texas Studies in English*, 34 (1955), 67–100; W. P. Albrecht, "Hazlitt's Preference for Tragedy," *PMLA*, 71 (1956), 1042–51; J. D. O'Hara, "Hazlitt and Romantic Criticism of the Fine Arts," *The Journal of Aesthetics and Art Criticism*, 27, No. 1 (Fall 1968), 73–85.

I

The Critical Setting

MUCH OF WHAT is significant and distinctive about Hazlitt's literary theory and criticism can be fully understood only in terms of its background and setting. From one viewpoint, it sounds quite traditional, developing and utilizing such concepts and themes as imagination, intuition, taste, sympathy, association, and disinterestedness which had achieved considerable currency in the eighteenth century. For Wellek, Hazlitt "is, like Wordsworth, rooted in the English empiricist tradition, and like Wordsworth he inherits the emotionalism and Rousseauism of the later 18th century."[1] Elizabeth Schneider sees him as "a product of eighteenth-century 'common sense' " who "had taken the eighteenth century with him when he entered the nineteenth."[2]

From another viewpoint, particularly when seen in company with critics like Wordsworth, Coleridge, Lamb, and Shelley, his theory and criticism seems to represent a fresh new beginning for criticism and indeed for literature. Its strongly emotional foundations, its scorn of abstraction and generalization, its image of nature as a fluid process of great richness and complexity, its advocacy of imagination as a truly creative and shaping faculty which alone can represent the truth of reality—these and so many other emphases seem to represent the sharpest kind of break with the critical tradition. As one of Hazlitt's earliest commentators rhapsodically puts it, the critic started a new kind of criticism. "He is less a writer than an illustrator, and less an illustrator than an enthusiastic expositor and panegyrist, whose eulogium is the spontaneous overflow of an exquisite perception of, and an intense sympathy with, the beauties on which he expatiates."[3]

And yet neither of these viewpoints is completely in tune with Hazlitt's actual criticism and with the specific context in which it was thought out and written. It is as if one needs both to come to any kind of understanding of Hazlitt's place in the history of criticism, of what is old and what is new about his several positions, and of what his real contribution is to the theory and practice of criticism. His work, on the one hand, is solidly grounded in Hobbes, Locke, and the British empirical tradition, and yet, on the other, offers a sharp rejoinder to that tradition. His critical position shows the impact of Shaftesbury, Hutcheson, and the ideals of the School of Taste and Sentimentalism, and yet it is critical of those criteria of emotionalism which are rooted solely in the individual and are neglectful of the larger reality beyond. Professor Bate suggests a possible methodology when dealing with the entire concept of the Romantic imagination in the early-nineteenth century. "Where it is most successful and informative," he contends, "the romantic conception of the imagination simply assumes and expands the theory of mind that was developed during the eighteenth century by English empirical psychology—a theory of mind that had supported and had developed along with the empirical emphasis on concrete, particularized nature. Of its application to romantic values in literary criticism, Hazlitt is the most notable example."[4]

In short, the student of Hazlitt must, as far as possible, see the eighteenth century as a backdrop for Hazlitt's critical efforts, but he must see it, not as the monolithic structure all too easily described as "The Age of Reason," but rather as a period of remarkable variety within a framework revealing a basic faith in certain ideals such as order, reason, restraint, and decorum. B. H. Bronson's graphic analysis of the period—

the emotional ferment, the resistance to rule, the communion with external nature, all those signs and signals of "Romanticism" that complicate the *opening* of the Age of Reason; next, the irregular and disconcertingly rhythmless horizon line where at unpredictable intervals the different arts thrust up their temporal peaks; and, toward the close of the century, the passion for order, the lofty vision of a timeless beauty, the powerful affirmations of faith in man's ability to define and by strenuous effort to approximate it by the rational use of his human endowment, his shared inheritance, native and natural: the persistent and lasting devotion to the Classical Ideal

—is a searching and suggestive one for all of us tempted by the great Seductress, the History of Ideas, or by what Professor Bronson calls "interpretation *ex post facto*."[5] Such a view may make possible an assessment of what in the eighteenth century attracted and repelled Hazlitt, and, more important, what peculiar impact he brought to those elements which he gathered, synthesized, and incorporated into his work. It is in this last area that I feel Hazlitt is most original and most influential, for in the happy combination of what he found valuable in the tradition of Neoclassicism and what the unique force of his own genius brought to this tradition there is something approaching the emergence of a new aesthetic and a new criticism.

Hazlitt reveals throughout his work a keen sensitivity to the many changes in eighteenth-century literature and thought; indeed, it is the period whose intellectual and artistic achievements he seems to know best. Rarely is he given to caricature. He knows its dominant thrusts and its unorthodox and liberal currents; he knows the exemplars of the tradition and the mavericks. He recognizes that no such thing as an Augustan harmony ever prevailed, that even in the heyday of the English Enlightenment a significant number of philosophers and artists were almost totally out of sympathy with prevailing ideals. Indeed, one should read his criticism with an awareness of certain dominant emphases of the previous age, emphases which should be discussed at the outset of this study.

The return of Charles II to the throne of England in 1660 after the violence and chaos of the Puritan Revolution assumed a kind of symbolic significance for enlightened Englishmen. To some it was like the return of Augustus Caesar to Rome after the Civil Wars, celebrated in great occasional poems like Dryden's *Astraea Redux*, and was regarded as a restoration not only of political order, but of intellectual harmony after the excesses of Puritan enthusiasm. There was the expectation of a new era of "sweet reasonableness." Even when disillusionment and cynicism followed the revelation of Charles as a slothful and unresourceful king who brought back, not the peace of Augustus, but the epicureanism of France, there was the feeling nonetheless that a new era had dawned and that reasonable men ought to begin a new quest for harmony rooted not in emotion or religious feeling, but in a more rational approach to man and the world. With figures like Bacon and Descartes as intellectual forebears, the vision of a new society and a new way of life seemed like more than a possibility. As Peter Gay contends,

> Since Bacon's utilitarian empiricism did not essentially conflict with Descartes's severe mathematical intellectuality, it followed that in the sciences the most highly developed rationality was also the most useful. In fact, Bacon's and Descartes's ideas on method converged because they agreed on the true purpose of philosophy: the end of true philosophizing was mastery over nature. "The true and lawful goal of the sciences," wrote Bacon, "is none other than this: that human life be endowed with new discoveries and powers."[6]

Paralleling this rationalistic bent was the continuing growth of and enthusiasm for natural science. "Impelled by the imperatives of the scientific discipline, excited by new discoveries, new instruments, and the free international commerce of information, the natural philosophers proclaimed themselves new men, pioneers without ancestors, superior to all the ancients."[7] The Royal Society, whose leading members included Robert Boyle in chemistry, John Ray in natural science, and Isaac Newton in mathematics and astronomy, became a symbol of the new learning and the new intellectual posture. The Society's concern was not simply with the special problems of science and philosophy, but also with such matters as language and expression, one of its major aims being the reformation of English style after the excesses of the seventeenth century. Bishop Thomas Sprat, in his *History of the Royal Society*, wrote of the great need for a certain clarity, simplicity, and ease in writing, qualities which Hobbes also encouraged. The great trend was toward simplification and away from mystery and wonder. The experimental method was increasingly stressed as Aristotle was downgraded more and more as a student of natural phenomena. The great focus was on the concrete reality within which man lives and moves and has his being, and on science as the vehicle of progress.

One might say that from 1660 until approximately the middle of the next century something like intellectual harmony prevailed in the world of English Neoclassicism, generating a fairly widespread attitude that men were beginning anew after the excesses of pre-Restoration emotionalism and discord, that the new era could become a model of the new reason and science after the literary chaos of Metaphysical poetry and the political and social turbulence of the Puritan Revolution. A new and basically realistic conservatism became the antidote for Puritan outspokenness and individualism, and actual behavior much more the focus of attention than theorizing or metaphysical speculation. A kind of consensus morality evolved, with the judgment of one's group becoming the source of wisdom. So many sections of Pope's *Essay on Criticism* capture the spirit, especially the following:

> For as in bodies, thus in souls, we find
> What wants in blood and spirits, swell'd with wind:

> Pride, where wit fails, steps into our defence,
> And fills up all the mighty void of sense.
> If once right reason drives that cloud away,
> Truth breaks upon us with resistless day.
> Trust not yourself; but your defects to know,
> Make use of every friend—and every foe.
>   A little learning is a dangerous thing;
> Drink deep or taste not the Pierian spring;
> There shallow draughts intoxicate the brain,
> And drinking largely sobers us again.

Citing Locke's strong influence on the age, Gerald R. Cragg develops succinctly this strong strain of realism in the thought of the period. "The fact," he suggests,

> that Locke's detailed analysis of reason is open to criticism is, for our purposes, beside the point. The importance which he attached to reason and the general character of his treatment of it were authoritative for the eighteenth century. He taught his successors the value of reflecting on ordinary experience and the necessity of subjecting it to careful scrutiny. This seemed to him much more important than framing ingenious theories. The common sense which he exemplified sometimes degenerated, in the hands of others, into an exposition of the prudential wisdom of the average man. But this was not what Locke commended; he urged upon his contemporaries the need of careful reflection on ordinary experience.[8]

Underlying this new and relatively narrow norm of realism was a confidence, rooted perhaps in Descartes' *Discourse on Method*, that the law of reason had been restored, that the mind had been cleared of cant, and that men, in agreement on certain basic principles, could move toward more general agreement on a wider range of human experience. The new emphasis was on common, as opposed to individual, experience, and it received its most telling and influential statement in the great bible of English Neoclassic thought, John Locke's *Essay Concerning Human Understanding* (1690).

The two great watchwords of the period were Nature and Reason, both extremely ambivalent in their implications. The great guide of life and of literature was Nature conceived as the wondrous order of the universe, as a stable, static, "Great Machine, working by rigidly determined laws of material causation."[9] What stands out most clearly in so many major treatments of Nature in this period is its constancy—to use Pope's famous expression "One clear, unchanged, and universal light"—not its variety and complexity. The seventeenth century, it will be recalled, made no strong appeal to natural law; the Puritans, for example, had regarded philosophy as suspect and had raised Revelation to a position of pre-eminence. After the Puritan demise, however, and especially in the years after the Restoration, Revelation became the great object of suspicion, and the new empirico-rationalistic attitude emerged, with the concept of Nature at its center. Nature now is something distinct from Revelation, the appeal to which had generated only vain speculation, controversy, and religious warfare. It is the superb order of created things, a standard of excellence created by a Deistic Great Architect God and revealing in its many processes evidences of that God. It is also a pattern of order incorporating human nature and providing man with a clear image of himself, his relationship to other aspects of the pattern, and his responsibility and standard of conduct in view of his position in the scheme of things. Reason is the Lockean *tabula rasa*, the relatively passive recipient of impressions from experience, a storehouse of a kind of cumulative wisdom which becomes the guide of human action and the source of great art. Pope's words, this time in the *Essay on Man*, admirably capture this spirit:

> All are but parts of one stupendous whole,
> Whose body Nature is, and God the soul;
> That, changed through all, and yet in all the same;

> Great in the earth, as in the ethereal frame;
> Warms in the sun, refreshes in the breeze,
> Glows in the stars, and blossoms in the trees,
> Lives through all life, extends through all extent,
> Spreads undivided, operates unspent;
> Breathes in our soul, informs our mortal part,
> As full, as perfect, in a hair as heart;
> As full, as perfect in vile man that mourns,
> As the rapt seraph that adores and burns:
> To him no high, no low, no great, no small;
> He fills, He bounds, connects, and equals all.
>   Cease then, nor order imperfection name:
> Our proper bliss depends on what we blame.
> Know thy own point: this kind, this due degree
> Of blindness, weakness, Heaven bestows on thee.

Indeed, these were the great years of natural religion, Blake's *bête noire*, which seemed to push supernatural faith, Revelation, the wonderful, and the mysterious into the background and to search for more concrete proofs of God's existence in the magnificent manifestations of an orderly universe. Burnet's *Sacred Theory of the Earth* and Derham's *Physico-Theology* are but two of the inquiries seeking God in his creation.

More and more of the older Renaissance image of an order linking all things, natural and supernatural, was eroded. Newton and Locke were the promulgators of the new gospel of nature and man. According to Professor Cragg, Locke "acknowledged that some truths are above reason—though never contrary to it. He allowed a place for the supernatural order and for divine revelation. But he was a rationalist in that he insisted that all truths must ultimately be judged by reason, and he viewed with deep distrust any attempt to override its verdict."[10]

Within this Deistic framework man stands as the great master endowed with the power to know nature and the truth. His great goal is, through his faculty of reason, to behold and understand the wisdom of God in the creation.

Such a reason-governed outlook underlay many of the age's attitudes toward man, religion, morality, and government. The exaltation of Nature and Reason was typical of much English Neoclassicism, and many derivative beliefs followed. The ideal or typical or universal, to be known through reason, became the criterion of taste. Rules, method, were the proper means of achieving this criterion. These rules are most perfectly embodied in the ancient writers, particularly those of Augustan Rome, who had so well manifested the order of Nature in their works. In the rigid, mechanistic theory of the post-Restoration years, a kind of Neoclassical doctrine emerged, rooted in ideas popular much earlier in Italy and France and familiar in England in the writings of Sir Philip Sidney and Ben Jonson. Many of these rules, concerning the genres, the unities, imitation, and the like, were actually second- or third-hand versions of classical theory interpreted in the dogmatizing spirit of contemporary commentators. Mere suggestions and counsels became critical doctrine in these commentators; the spirit seemed more Horatian than Aristotelian. Sterner critics and theorists such as Davenant, Hobbes, and Rymer revealed a strict traditionalism which placed a high premium on imitating the ancients and following the rules embodied in their works. Theirs was a strongly empirical and rationalistic bent which forcefully urged the values of judgment and probability in art and expressed a decided caution with regard to such matters as original genius, imaginative eccentricity, and individual creativity. Art, and specifically literature, were ancillary in purpose; the key goals were moral edification, common sense, and propriety.

Sir William Davenant's prefatory epistle to *Gondibert* (1660) conceived of the poet, not as a man of strong passions, a shaper of personal experience, a creator of symbol, but rather as a lawgiver committed to verisimilitude and probability. Ever a hater of imaginative excess, Hobbes regarded art as chiefly psychological and rhetorical, a vehicle of persuasion. According to his psychology, the mind is divided into wit, or invention, his terminology for quickness in imagining; disposition or judgment, which is the great faculty of control; and eloquence, which is associated with the ornaments of poetry. The basic distinction is between wit, the associating and combining faculty, and judgment, the discerning and differentiating faculty—a distinction which in one form or another became central in eighteenth-century criticism, especially in the famous comparisons like Dryden's of Shakespeare and Ben Jonson, Pope's of Homer and Vergil, and even Johnson's of Dryden and Pope. Wit is in every way a lesser faculty which must be subordinated to the overseeing activity of the judgment.

Even in the more humane, liberal, and sophisticated criticism of great figures like Dryden, Pope, and Johnson the basic critical conservatism of the age can be seen. Pope's version of the composition of the *Aeneid* and of Vergil's discovery, just at the point when "he seemed above the critic's law" and "but from Nature's fountains scorned to draw," that Nature and Homer were the same, sets the Neoclassic ideal of imitation of models in wonderfully sharp perspective. To poets and critics like Dryden and Pope, generous in their praise of the exuberance of Chaucer, Shakespeare, Homer, and other non-Neoclassic types, the ancients had nevertheless provided a body of artistic and critical models so sound and of such general application that those who came after needed only to follow them to be in conformity with Nature. Those who ignored them, in the name of spontaneity or individual expression, though they might "snatch a grace beyond the reach of art," nevertheless ignored them at their peril. "Between 1660 and 1800," argues James Johnson,

> a "classicist" was the man who saw within preserved Greco-Roman literature a total and applicable world. He was concerned with *all* of that literature as manifestation of a total world, geography as well as

epic, history and philosophy as well as satire. His fundamental introit was through the study of syntax and etymology, but once inside classical literature, the scholar's frame of mind was not simply "literary" but utilitarian. In time, a "classic" came to mean a masterwork of any period, though usually an ancient one, which exerted a cultural influence or which contained permanent, archetypal qualities. The "realities" of the contemporary world—whether social, political, military, literary, or moral—became more attainable through reading the "classics."[11]

While providing the contemporary artist with prototypes of artistic excellence, these ancient models also contributed to a kind of creative paralysis, as the poet confronted what Walter Jackson Bate has described as the "burden of the past" and wondered whether there were any new frontiers to explore, any new creative veins to tap, or whether the major function of genius is "What oft was thought, but ne'er so well expressed."[12]

With reason as the supreme faculty and imitation as a proper posture for the poet, the importance of the imagination and the emotions was minimized. Beginning with the Hobbesian idea of the imagination as "decaying sense" and continuing through Samuel Johnson's warning about imagination as a "licentious vagrant faculty, unsusceptible of limitations and restraint," there was a pronounced wariness about the dominance of this faculty in life and in art and, consequently, a tendency, not to ignore it, but to subordinate it to reason, to the direct observation and representation of reality. "Wit," as it was called in so many discussions, was the handmaiden of "judgment," the adorner of truth, and as such not a guiding or formative faculty in the whole creative process. As with the faculty, so also with its creations, whether similes or metaphors. These figures of speech, though enormously useful in their rhetorical role of rendering reality more attractive or truth more palatable, must, in Horace's words, be "non nova sed nove," must not challenge credibility by moving too far from the reality which they represent. Dryden's strong emphasis on a pure and denotative language; Pope's "Expression is the dress of thought"; Johnson's praise of Pope's simile of the Alps in the *Essay on Criticism* because it "has no useless parts, yet affords a striking picture by itself; it makes the foregoing position better understood, and enables it to take faster hold of the attention; it assists the apprehension and elevates the fancy," and his indictment of the Metaphysical poets because their "thoughts are often new but seldom natural; they are not obvious, but neither are they just; and the reader, far from wondering that he missed them, wonders more frequently by what perverseness of industry they were ever found"—all are familiar cases in point. As M. H. Abrams writes,

> Through most of the eighteenth century, the poet's invention and imagination were made thoroughly dependent for their materials—their ideas and "images"—on the external universe and the literary models the poet had to imitate; while the persistent stress laid on his need for judgment and art—the mental surrogates, in effect, of the requirements of a cultivated audience—held the poet strictly responsible to the audience for whose pleasure he exerted his creative ability.[13]

A similarly conservative approach governed many eighteenth-century discussions of emotion and feeling in the human situation as well as in artistic endeavor. Again, as was the case with imagination, this is not to suggest that there was not a tremendous concern with the role of emotion; indeed, as the century progressed, it was the concern which seriously weakened the prevailing rationalistic outlook of the age. What one notes is a greater emphasis on restraint, on decorum and propriety, and on feeling, not as a dominant principle as a work of art, but as operating within a larger framework of reason and control. Although there is praise in Dryden, Pope, Johnson, and others for strongly individualistic genius, for Homer, Chaucer, Shakespeare, for spontaneity and passion in works of art, there is always the higher praise for the more self-conscious, conservative, traditional artists like Vergil, Ben Jonson, and Pope himself. The original genius, the autobiographical poet, whose work is an outpouring of his most deeply felt emotions, the work of art as personal experience—all these might have been regarded as interesting phenomena, but they were nevertheless exemplifications of a peculiar psychological imbalance, of feeling gaining the ascendancy over reason and judgment.

Nature, for so many major writers of the period, is not so much the concrete, vital, and dynamic world of natural beauty, of sea, sky, forest, and mountain, in which man is a participant, as a regular, static creation of which man is a somewhat detached spectator.

The effects of such a climate on the literature and the criticism of the age were very great. Although generalization is dangerous in view of the great variety of artistic endeavor, certain things stand out very clearly. Particularly evident in much of the literature is a lack of spontaneity, of directly expressed and strongly individual feeling, and an underplaying of the wonderful and the mysterious as objects of serious concern. The Neoclassic years are memorable for a greater concern with prose than with poetry. The poetry prizes abstraction and generality, and seems less concerned with the concretizing power of the imagination and with the expression of individual emotion.[14] The predominance of satire in the writing of Dryden, Pope, and Swift; the great growth of critical writing; the enormous popularity of the periodical essay—these and other fashions seem admirably suited to the spirit of an age and an audience interested in sensibleness, clarity, and elegant commonplaces with a minimum of metaphysical speculation and creative urgency. According to James Sutherland, Samuel Johnson's poetry "was more deliberately submitted to the public. The eighteenth-century poet's consciousness of this public inhibited the expression of emotion, unless it was of a recognized and acceptable kind. It is absurd to contend that eighteenth-century poetry is lacking in feeling; it is still more naïve to suppose that the poets of that century did not feel as men."[15] There is an interesting self-consciousness, indeed defensiveness, in a good deal of Neoclassic poetry, reflecting poets' uncertainty about their role in society and their consequent desire to bring poetry closer to prose in its method or to make poetry serve some practical purpose. Goldsmith's *The Deserted Village*, Pope's *Essay on Criticism*, and Darwin's *The Botanic Garden* are but a few examples of this poetic stance. Poets tended to value strongly qualities of clarity, order, and common sense. Dryden, although not escaping completely what he criticized harshly, sought to restore the purity of the English language after the aberrations of Metaphysical poetry; Pope complained that in contemporary poetry "Words are like leaves, and where they most abound, / Much fruit of sense beneath is rarely found"; while Johnson, unhappy with what he felt reduced "strength of thought to happiness of language," sought "a more noble and adequate conception" of wit as that "which is at once natural and new."

The iambic pentameter couplet, the tight, closed, disciplined form, became the perfect vehicle for a certain concentration, conciseness, and epigrammatic quality. Generally speaking, there is a very strong rhetorical posture in the poetry; it eschews the poem as the spontaneous expression of deeply personal emotion and communicates a public and social tone which almost always seems conscious of and responsive to an audience. A clear and denotative diction; a balanced, smooth sentence structure; a vigorous and rhythmic movement—these are some of the cherished aims of poetic style. The simile, a more controlled figure of speech relatively free from too great a range of complexity and suggestion, is preferred to the metaphor with its compression and consequent ambivalence.

External nature, not in its wilder, more undomesticated manifestations, but as touched by man, was the poet's chief concern. Excessive enthusiasm for the concrete beauties of nature was looked upon as symptomatic of a prevalence of feeling over reason. To Samuel Johnson the study of man's ideals and conduct was considered kinship with nature. To Alexander Pope nature was more than sea, sky, or mountain; it was nature modified by human action. This is not in any way to suggest that eighteenth-century poetry is exclusively a poetry of the indoors. From Dryden forward, all kinds of poems dealt with the varied beauties of nature beyond the country estate or the city mansion. James Sutherland observes that the caricature

> that the eighteenth-century poet was less observant than the average Boy Scout of the twentieth century is one that will not bear examination: if he did not fill his poems with sharply individualized descriptions of nature it must have been—it was—because he considered that as a poet something more difficult and more profitable was expected of him. From his own varied experience he distilled those elements which appeared to him to be common to all individual instances.[16]

It would, of course, as suggested earlier, be folly to view the eighteenth century as in any sense monolithic, in spite of the main currents of thought considered above, and Bronson's warning about such descriptions of the age remains a salutary one. Despite the prevailing attitudes, attitudes to which Hazlitt was extremely sensitive, the seeds of change always seemed present, and all I can do in a short space is to suggest some of the variety, especially as it bears on the evolution of his criticism.

One of the most significant aspects of Anglo-Scottish literary theory, especially of the middle- and late-eighteenth century, was the pronounced concern with the operations of the human mind, with the effect of art on the reader or spectator, and with the means of achieving this particular effect. So also there was a growing loss of concern with the criticism of literature on traditional and formalistic grounds. Artists and critics alike reveal an increasing weariness with the didactic and the moralistic, with the notion that mere regularity is a thing to be praised. Joseph Warton's relegation of Pope's poetry to the second order is an interesting case in point.

They bring to their work an increased awareness and conviction that sensation and imagination are significant conduits of knowledge, that strong feeling and freedom from restraints are the foundations of great art. As W. J. Bate contends, such tendencies are indicative that "critical theory followed the lead of formal empirical psychology, and turned upon the mind itself, hoping, through psychological analysis, to discover at least some common principles of human feeling and human reaction by which some standard of taste could be roughly determined."[17] The sensationalism of Thomas Hobbes, the empiricism and strong anti-abstractionism of Locke, were pioneering forces in the development of the new experiential outlook which fascinated critics like Addison and poets like Akenside and culminated, although in different forms, in the writing of Hume and Hartley.

Another strong anti-rationalistic development of the age is the emotionalism associated with much eighteenth-century French and English thought and rooted in England in the work of Anthony Ashley Cooper, the third Earl of Shaftesbury. The image of an absolutely beneficent Deity, the strong emphasis on the individual, the doctrine of an inherent taste for beauty and virtue, the general shift to a feeling-governed approach to life and literature—these were the hallmarks not just of Shaftesbury but of Francis Hutcheson and a host of other sentimental theorists who anticipate the Romantic stress on the natural goodness of the individual and on the validity of feeling and intuition as modes of judgment.

New ideas of genius and sublimity stimulate an entirely new way of thinking about the true artist and his subject. A strong new examination of the creativity of the imagination reveals its powers of association, coalescence, and sympathy and a variety of other activities central to the artistic and critical process. Adam Smith, Lord Kames, Edmund Burke, Alexander Gerard, William Duff—these are but a few of the writers who come to mind as part of a force furthering the strongly subjective drift in British aesthetics fifty years before Wordsworth and Coleridge. The more practical criticism similarly reveals an interest in the novel, the sublime, and the passionate as effects of art, and documents like Edward Young's *Conjectures on Original Composition*, Thomas Warton's *Observations on Spenser's Faerie Queene*, Joseph Warton's *Essay on the Genius and Writings of Pope* reveal a fascinating process of dissatisfaction with contemporary literary reputations and a search for new objects of praise. More will be said about some of these writers later since they form a significant part of the psychological and critical education of William Hazlitt.

The development of literature, especially of poetry, during these years is equally notable. Poets, weary of aesthetic restraints, began to express strong feeling much more directly. Spontaneity became a quite positive value. Wild, undomesticated nature became more and more a familiar subject, and poems like Joseph Warton's *The Enthusiast*, Thomas Warton's *The Pleasure of Melancholy*, James Macpherson's *Ossian*, James Thompson's *The Seasons* are good examples. The imagination, unshackled from the intimidations of mechanistic controls and reveling in its powers of creativity, unveiled a world of refreshing beauty in Mark Akenside's *The Pleasures of Imagination*, in the odes of William Collins, and in many other lyric poems of the time. The search for new ways of justifying strong feelings led to the past to seek authority, and Percy's *Reliques of Ancient English Poetry*, Chatterton's medievalism, Macpherson's Scottish romance, Gray's interest in Norse sagas and Icelandic ballads, Horace Walpole's Gothicism expressed a restlessness with things as they are and a quest for wonder and mystery. Indeed, William Blake, whose work began in the eighteenth century, so turned away from Augustan rationalism and Newtonian positivism that he sought to create in his *Prophetic Books* a new world of myth in which the sacred power of Imagination triumphs over reason and re-creates a lost world of beauty and love.

Such is the age into which Hazlitt as a critic comes—strongly varied in its preoccupation with new ways of thinking and imagining, new modes of artistic expression, new ways of justifying the novel and the grotesque, new ways of talking about life and literature.

NOTES

1. René Wellek, *A History of Modern Criticism, 1750–1950*. II. *The Romantic Age* (New Haven: Yale University Press, 1955), p. 190.
2. *Aesthetics of William Hazlitt*, pp. 85, 86.
3. Ireland, *William Hazlitt*, p. 1.
4. *Criticism: The Major Texts*, ed. W. J. Bate (New York: Harcourt, Brace, 1952), p. 292.
5. "When Was Neoclassicism?" in *Studies in Criticism and Aesthetics, 1660–1800: Essays in Honor of Samuel Holt Monk*, edd. Howard P. Anderson and John S. Shea (Minneapolis: The University of Minnesota Press, 1967), p. 35.
6. *The Enlightenment: An Interpretation* (New York: Knopf, 1967), pp. 311–12.
7. Ibid., p. 308.
8. *Reason and Authority in the Eighteenth Century* (Cambridge: Cambridge University Press, 1964), p. 8.
9. Basil Willey, *The Eighteenth Century Background: Studies in the Thought of the Period* (London: Chatto & Windus, 1940), p. 4.
10. *Reason and Authority*, p. 8.
11. *The Formation of English Neo-Classical Thought* (Princeton: Princeton University Press, 1967), p. 29.
12. *The Burden of the Past and the English Poet* (Cambridge: The Belknap Press of Harvard University Press, 1970).
13. *The Mirror and the Lamp: Romantic Theory and the Critical Tradition* (New York: Oxford University Press, 1953), p. 21.

14. The recent studies of William H. Youngren on the whole question of generality in Restoration and eighteenth-century English literature are absolutely vital for a full understanding of this issue. See his "Generality in Augustan Satire," in *In Defense of Reading: A Reader's Approach to Literary Criticism*, edd. Reuben A. Brower and Richard Poirier (New York: Dutton, 1962), pp. 206–34; "Generality, Science and Poetic Language in the Restoration," *ELH*, 35 (1968), 158–87; and "Conceptualism and Neoclassic Generality," ibid., 47 (1980), 705–40.

15. *A Preface to Eighteenth Century Poetry* (Oxford: Clarendon, 1948), p. 67.

16. Ibid., p. 28.

17. *Criticism*, p. 271.

2

Intellectual Forebears

> Men's opinions and reasonings depend more on the
> character of their minds than we are apt to conceive.
> *Prospectus of a History of English Philosophy*
> [II 113]

THERE IS PERHAPS NO NEED for an elaborate intellectual genealogy of Hazlitt. A good deal of the recent scholarship on his aesthetics and criticism, as well as the excellent treatment of his life and times, have paid careful attention to the books he read, the philosophies he found congenial, the intellectual debates in which he was engaged. Elizabeth Schneider some years ago and Roy Park and John Kinnaird recently in particular have shown at great length the elements which they consider central in the development of a mind, of a way of dealing with basic questions of epistemology, of a method through which one can confront life and literature honestly and straightforwardly. So also have such students of Hazlitt as W. P. Albrecht, Herschel Baker, W. J. Bate, J. D. O'Hara, and Leonard Trawick. Almost all this scholarship has been in fundamental agreement on certain key aspects of Hazlitt's background: the vitality of the English tradition of Nonconformity, the early impact of the empirical philosophy of Hobbes and Locke and the later disenchantment with that philosophy, the significance of Rousseau, the general influence of the Anglo-Scottish psychologist–critics, the strong interest in idealist theories. Such studies have in most cases provided for one seriously interested in Hazlitt a great sense of a strong and fiercely individualistic man who responded to a wide variety of ideas and theories and who in the process developed certain striking habits of mind.

What needs special attention today, especially by one concerned with understanding Hazlitt's theory and its practical application to literary problems, is clear. The task is not so much to rehearse this wealth of materials as to seek out its dominant patterns and its key features, especially as these enable one to establish connections between Hazlitt's aesthetic theorizing and the method of his practical criticism. Consequently, the early phases of this study will not treat Hazlitt's intellectual forebears *de novo*, but rather will consider certain of their central premisses as they illuminate his modes of judgment.

The pattern of Nonconformity, for example, is fixed in his life at a very early stage.[1] Almost from the beginning there is the sense in his life and writing that he is in the minority, that he has been discriminated against, that he must take a stand for individual values, whether religious, political, or literary, against a fixed and insensitive establishment. He was quick to feel kinship with the Dissenters and to be impressed by heroes of Nonconformity like Joseph Priestley and Richard Price. His early attraction to republicanism and puritanism was the response of a young man feeling oppressed and eager to find a strong articulation of the rights of the individual. Yet he was no old-fashioned thinker merely restating familiar doctrines. Characteristic of his mode of assimilating what he considered valuable in older ideas and theories, his method was to update and recharge, to bring to bear his own fresh and personal ways of dealing with problems so that what finally emerged as an idea, a policy, a critique was very much his own. A good many years ago Sir Leslie Stephen saw one dimension of the process quite well:

> Like some others of his revolutionary friends, Godwin, for example, Leigh Hunt, and Tom Paine, he represents the old dissenting spirit in

a new incarnation. The grandfather a stern Calvinist, the father a Unitarian, the son a freethinker; those were the gradations through which more than one family passed during the closing years of the last century and the opening of this. One generation still clung to the old Puritan traditions and Jonathan Edwards; the next followed Priestley; and the third joined the little band of radicals who read Cobbett, scorned Southey as a deserter, and refused to be frightened by the French Revolution. The outside crust of opinion may be shed with little change to the inner man. Hazlitt was a dissenter to his backbone. He was born to be in a minority; to be a living protest against the dominant creed and constitution.[2]

In September of 1793, at the age of fifteen, Hazlitt entered the Unitarian New College in Hackney, one of the so-called Dissenting academies, as a divinity student.[3] Tom Paine and Joseph Priestley, two of the most outspoken freethinkers, were great favorites at the school, and Hazlitt attended Priestley's lectures. Stephenson speculates on "the boyish eagerness with which he would attend the first, and perhaps all, of the lectures which he heard from one for whom his father had high regard, one whose writings he himself had eagerly read when he was but a boy of twelve years of age, one whom he had eagerly defended in the *Shrewsbury Chronicle* when, after the Birmingham riots, his [Priestley's] name had been loaded with abuse."[4] Priestley left England for America, a kind of exile, but one whose lectures (published under the title *Heads of Lectures on a Course of Experimental Philosophy, particularly including Chemistry: delivered at the New College in Hackney*) and whose life became almost symbolic of Nonconformity to the students. As Stephenson puts it, "Probably, the young Hazlitt, intense as his reading may have been, was influenced most of all by the events of the day and the reactions to them in the minds of those with whom he was most nearly associated."[5] Hazlitt remained at Hackney until the summer of 1795, and it is fair to say that during his studies there he, like his fellow-radical William Godwin before him, grew to doubt the value of a life in the ministry, and his interests turned increasingly toward the arts.

Hazlitt's philosophical roots, in spite of his later recantation and protestation, were squarely in the British empirical tradition. His lifelong zest for concrete reality, for the vivid image, and for intense sensation, and his detestation of abstraction, theorizing, and categorization, although very much dimensions of his personality, nevertheless have specific connections with his early reading in philosophy. Professor Schneider recommends a healthy skepticism as to close parallels between his reading and his ideas, arguing that certain ideas are products not so much of his reading of a particular writer as of the popularizations which he encountered in the periodicals which he read constantly or of the conversations in which he participated.[6] At the same time the more one reads about the young Hazlitt and his intellectual interests, the more one is attracted by certain strains in his earliest reading, by particular concerns in his youthful speculations. While at Hackney, Professor Albrecht recounts, Hazlitt "read principally in what he called 'the material, or *modern* philosophy.' He learned a great deal from the empirical philosophers—especially from Hobbes, Locke, and Hartley."[7] The letters exchanged with his father while he was at school are quite interesting, particularly one in 1793 in which he speaks of reading "David Hartley."[8] Leonard Trawick contends that "the assumptions behind his thought, which he assimilated from Berkeley, Hume, Hartley, Priestley, Reid, Tucker, and others in whose writings he immersed himself, had their roots in Locke."[9] Hazlitt himself extended the empirical tradition back to Bacon whom he respected greatly and regarded, in spite of certain reservations, as "one of the wisest of mankind" (VI 326). Bacon he saw as a pioneering force in philosophy "in wishing to recall men's attention to facts and experience which had been almost entirely neglected" and in insisting on the "necessity of experience" (II 115).

Undoubtedly, reading in philosophers like Bacon, Hobbes, Locke, Hume, and Hartley directed his attention away from the vagaries of metaphysical speculation, and pointed toward the empirical approach with its emphasis on the nature and workings of the mind and the limitations of its experience. The grandeur of concrete experience, its naked reality, its continuing varieties and contrasts; the centrality of sensation and association in any theory of knowledge; the dangers of ratiocination—these were essential tenets of the young man's earliest credo.

Yet as formative as this tradition was in his youthful development, Hazlitt was quick to criticize what he considered its limitations as he matured. He increasingly found himself unable to accept the notion of the mind as passive, as a mere gathering-place of sensations. He was, in Professor Albrecht's words, "repelled by their mechanistic conception of the mind and by their self-centered, necessitarian morality."[10] It is this repulsion which is revealed so clearly in his *Lectures on English Philosophy* and, most important, in his *Essay on the Principles of Human Action*. In spite of his enormous respect for Bacon, that philosopher is nevertheless the source of a most constricting psychology, limiting experience to "a knowledge of things without us," and concluding that "all thought is to be resolved into sensation, all morality into the love of pleasure, and all action into mechanical impulse" (II 124). The contemporary extremes of Bacon's position are obvious: "We despised experience altogether before: now we would have nothing but experience, and that of the grossest kind" (II 115). Hobbes "was by nature a materialist," and the "external image pressed so close upon his mind that it destroyed the power of consciousness, and left no room for attention to any thing but itself" (II 126). Locke, despite greater sophistication and careful qualification of Hobbes's blunt sensationalism, still reveals marked limitations. He is "so bent on exploding innate ideas, and tracing our thoughts to their external source, that he either forgot or had not leisure to examine what the internal principle of all thought is" (II 147). In his *Essay on the Principles of Human Action*, Hazlitt complains of the mechanistic approaches of Hartley and Helvétius, which make the mind a captive of external reality, and argues quite cogently that "the aggregate of many actual sensations is, we here plainly see, a totally different thing from the collective idea, comprehension, or *consciousness* of those sensations as many things, or of any of their relations to each other. We may go on multiplying and combining sensations to the end of time without ever advancing one step in the other process, or producing one single thought" (I 69).

What one observes is a most interesting middle ground in Hazlitt's thinking on epistemological questions. On the one hand, there is a strong empirical leaning; yet, on the other, there is a definite emphasis on the need for generalization as long as the mind in its processes of operation never loses its firm anchor in the materials of reality. He stressed especially the faculty of understanding as the real source of ideas, "a common principle of thought, a superintending faculty, which alone perceives the relations of things, and enables us to comprehend their connexions, forms, and masses" (II 151). Such a principle is at the root of man's reasonableness.

He was, of course, just as critical of the idealists and abstractionists, those who would find truth in a form or idea which transcends concrete reality. His remarks on Reynolds are perhaps the most sharply critical and might well stand for his rather consistent position on the subject. Reynolds, he contended, appeared to have imbibed a strange principle that art was to be preferred to nature and learning to genius. He further argued that Reynolds would merge the details of individual objects in order to secure a general effect and "is resolved to reduce all beauty or grandeur in natural objects to a central form or abstract idea of a certain class, so as to exclude all peculiarities or deviations from this ideal standard as unfit subjects for the artist's pencil, and as polluting his canvas with deformity" (VIII 137). Roy Park strongly emphasizes the point that Hazlitt saw himself chiefly as a painter and a philosopher until 1814 and that the combination underlies his antipathy to abstraction as he begins his career as a literary critic in 1814.[11]

Yet, although generalization and abstraction are inadequate modes of knowing, no reasonable creature can carry on the ordinary discourse of life without the ability to generalize, to articulate relationships and associations. "I hate people," he said, "who have no notion of any thing but generalities, and forms, and creeds, and naked propositions, even worse than I dislike those who cannot for the soul of them arrive at the comprehension of an abstract idea" (XII 44). The secret is in the kind of thought by which ideas are developed, and it is one in which ideas are constantly seen in relation to the fertile and varied universe of things.

Another quite significant strain in Hazlitt's thought is the emotionalism associated with much eighteenth-century French and English philosophy, and calling to mind Rousseau in France and Anthony Ashley Cooper, the third Earl of Shaftesbury, in England, an emotionalism which found its culmination in the poetry of Wordsworth. Such a philosophy, strongly anti-Lockean in thrust, advanced the idea of innate mental faculties, with Shaftesbury arguing for an internal moral sense and his disciple Francis Hutcheson advancing the implications of this doctrine for aesthetics with his idea of a faculty of beauty.[12] Both Shaftesbury and Hutcheson are strong in their praise of spontaneity and of the power of intuition to cut through the web of fact and logic to grasp essential truth in a vitally emotional way. Professor Schneider contends that the "reading of Rousseau at an early age fortified, if it did not determine, the bent of Hazlitt's mind in its emphasis upon 'feeling,' "[13] although, as will be shown later, he came to criticize severely that norm as a goal in itself and argued strongly for disinterestedness and sympathy as greater guides to moral action.

From a more purely aesthetic point of view, Hazlitt seems quite squarely in the mainstream of eighteenth-century Anglo-Scottish psychological theory. That fascinating complex of aesthetics, criticism, and philosophy has only recently begun to receive proper attention through discussions of a variety of concepts like genius, subjectivity, taste, imagination, and sympathy. Documents such as

Francis Hutcheson's *An Inquiry into the Originall of Our Ideas of Beauty and Virtue* (1725), David Hume's philosophical and literary essays (1739–1776), Adam Smith's *The Theory of Moral Sentiments* (1759), Lord Kames' *Elements of Criticism* (1762), Thomas Reid's *Inquiry into the Human Mind on the Principles of Common Sense* (1764), and Dugald Stewart's *Elements of the Philosophy of the Human Mind* (1792–1827) are important parts of that tradition. All seem dedicated to the undermining of rationalism, and, with Hume leading the way, to setting up a sense of sympathy, based on association, from which moral values could be educed.

Hazlitt knew an enormous amount of eighteenth-century philosophical writing; his works are "full of faculties, sensations, qualities, motives, and trains of association."[14] He had read Hume and Smith; in fact, he was reading Hume's *Treatise on Human Nature* in 1798, the year of his first meeting with Coleridge and at a time when he was working on his *Essay on the Principles of Human Action*. He is convinced that "there has been no metaphysician in this country worth the name" since Hume (VIII 65). Hume, Smith, and Hazlitt all concluded that sympathy, rooted in the imagination, is a key in human response. Hazlitt consistently deplored both the mechanistic psychology which made mind exclusively dependent upon sensation and the Hobbesian theory which made man little more than a self-serving brute. He similarly found inadequate and dangerous the idealism of Coleridge and Kant, ridiculing Coleridge's obscurantism (XI 32–34), and calling Kant's system "the most wilful and monstrous absurdity that ever was invented" (XVI 123). He sought and developed in his own thinking an image of the mind as creative, as beginning with the materials of experience but as molding from them new images, new realities. His admiration for Abraham Tucker led him to abridge Tucker's *Light of Nature Pursued* in 1807, praising its clarity of apprehension, its great insight into human nature, its overall common sense. For Hazlitt, Tucker "convinces the reader oftener by shewing him the thing in dispute, than by defining its abstract qualities; as the philosopher is said to have proved the existence of motion by getting up and walking" (1 124).

Hazlitt sought to justify the urgency of individual creativity, the superiority of genius to rules, the powers of association and coalescence, the centrality of taste in critical judgment. He clung to the vision of man as naturally disinterested, as most fully human when he goes out of himself to sympathize with others and to act accordingly. So much of this vision, which to be sure is uniquely his own, grew out of his great familiarity with eighteenth-century thought.

The preceding merely suggests the variety of ideas to which Hazlitt was exposed and to which he responded during his formative years and before he began his rather frantic career as a critic. Yet, as has been suggested, there are certain underlying attitudes about experience, the human mind, knowledge, artistic creation, and a host of other concerns which point up a dramatic shift from the broad emphases of the previous age as we have considered them. In a sense, all the elements for a new kind of criticism were ready; what was needed was a new kind of practicing critic, brash, enthusiastic, and eager to communicate directly his own experience with the world of art. Such a critic was Hazlitt.

NOTES

1. For an especially full treatment of this topic, see Herschel Baker, *William Hazlitt* (Cambridge: The Belknap Press of Harvard University Press, 1962), pp. 3–36.
2. "William Hazlitt," p. 239.

3. For much of the material in this section, I am indebted to H. W. Stephenson's valuable *William Hazlitt and Hackney College* (London: Lindsey, 1930).

4. Ibid., p. 24.

5. Ibid., p. 37.

6. *Aesthetics of William Hazlitt*, pp. 7–8.

7. *Hazlitt and the Creative Imagination* (Lawrence: The University of Kansas Press, 1965), p. 1.

8. *Lamb and Hazlitt: Further Letters and Records Hitherto Unpublished*, ed. William Carew Hazlitt (New York: Dodd, Mead, 1899), p. 35.

9. "Eighteenth Century Influences on the Criticism of William Hazlitt," Ph.D. Diss., Harvard University, 1961, p. 59.

10. *Hazlitt and the Creative Imagination*, p. 1.

11. *Hazlitt and the Spirit of the Age: Abstraction and Critical Theory* (Oxford: Clarendon, 1971), p. 96.

12. Trawick, "Eighteenth Century Influences," p. 8.

13. *Aesthetics of William Hazlitt*, p. 36.

14. Trawick, "Eighteenth Century Influences," p. 14.

3

A New Image of the Critic

BEFORE ONE CAN ADEQUATELY CONSIDER specific issues and themes in Hazlitt's criticism, it is vital to deal with the underlying spirit of that criticism. How did Hazlitt see himself and his craft? How would he compare himself to a Samuel Johnson or a Sir Joshua Reynolds, to a Cleanth Brooks, an Edmund Wilson, or a Northrop Frye? What was his conception of the fundamental business of criticism? This question of self-image and of the spirit which it generates is so radically distinctive in Hazlitt, so notably different from previous conceptions, and, indeed, from many modern views of the activity of the critic, that it should receive careful attention.

Hazlitt did not view himself as a seer or a lawgiver promulgating rules for the work of art and testing plays, poems, and novels by these rules. The older image of the self-conscious critic, aware of the tradition and weighing art in the context of that tradition, held little appeal for him. Nor, it would seem, did the more contemporary image of the systematic, analytic critic, working closely with texts and their implications, bringing to bear as he proceeds the tools of anthropology, history, sociology, linguistics, and a host of other disciplines. He was generally most unhappy with the idea of criticism as a negative activity, as a process of discovering and pointing up the failings of artists and writers. Verbal critics, as he calls them, are "mere word-catchers, fellows that pick out a word in a sentence and a sentence in a volume, and tell you it is wrong"; they are determined to "set you down lower than their opinion of themselves" (VIII 226). In *A View of the English Stage* he took an interesting line as he discussed some of his fellow-critics:

> We are aware that there is a class of connoisseurs whose envy it might be prudent to disarm, by some compromise with their perverted taste; who are horror-struck at grace and beauty, and who can only find relief and repose in the consoling thoughts of deformity and defect; whose blood curdles into poison at deserved reputation, who shudder at every temptation to *admire*, as an unpardonable crime, and shrink from whatever gives delight to others, with more than monkish self-denial [v 195].

He was impatient with the modern tendency toward elaborate analysis and explication, toward a fascination with multiple interpretations so that the "critic does nothing now-a-days who does not try to torture the most obvious expression into a thousand meanings, and enter into a circuitous explanation of all that can be urged for or against its being in the best or worst style possible. His object indeed is not to do justice to his author, whom he treats with very little ceremony, but to do himself homage, and to show his acquaintance with all the topics and resources of criticism" (VIII 214). Historical, philosophical, and formalistic critics do not fare much better; he spoke of the "cavillers" for whom "the author must be reduced to a class, all the living or defunct examples of which must be characteristically and pointedly *differenced* from one another; the value of this class of writing must be developed and ascertained in comparison with others; the principles of taste, the elements of our sensations, the structure of the human faculties, all must undergo a strict scrutiny and revision" (VIII 217).

The tendency in his own time toward sensational criticism has had, in Hazlitt's mind, very bad effects. A host of talented, but shallow, critics seek the shocking and the spectacular effect in the hope of gathering around them a special clique of followers. To these critics the basic values of a work of art are of relatively minor importance compared to "keeping up the character of the work and supplying the town with a sufficient number of grave or brilliant topics for the consumption of the next three months!" (VIII 216).

Most troubling are the obscurantist critics, the "*Occult School— verè adepti,*" as he described them. The obvious, the simply beautiful and delightful—all these are secondary to those who "discern no beauties but what are concealed from superficial eyes, and overlook all that are obvious to the vulgar part of mankind. . . . If an author is utterly unreadable, they can read him for ever: his intricacies are their delight, his mysteries are their study." Preferring Sir Thomas Browne to Dr. Johnson's *Rambler*, and Burton's *Anatomy of Melancholy* to all the writers of the Georgian Age, they hoard works of great genius as their special treasure which "is of no value unless they have it all to themselves" (VIII 225).

There is a similar freshness in Hazlitt's attempt to define and describe in new ways the proper operation of the critical mind as it deals with life and literature as evolving phenomena. Much as he admired Samuel Johnson, he nevertheless criticized him as essentially an unpoetical mind and hence as incapable of dealing adequately with the major challenges of imaginative works of art. Johnson's basic cast of mind dominated his critical instincts; his ideas were too determined by rule and system. His was a consecutive mind capable of grasping general principles and the main flow of human events, but it could not "shew how the nature of man was modified by the workings of passion, or the infinite fluctuations of thought and accident" (IV 175). His criticism is not just wrongheaded; it is dangerous. In a sense it was part of the mind of his age, which was in doubt about poetry, ambivalent about imaginative literature and its possibilities for the enlargement of the intellectual and emotional capacities of human beings. His analysis of Johnson and indeed of the dominant eighteenth-century attitude toward the arts is both penetrating and fascinating. Johnson lacks "any particular fineness of organic sensibility" and "that intenseness of passion, which, [seeks] to exaggerate whatever excites the feelings of pleasure or power in the mind." Consequently aesthetic considerations are consistently subservient, and "he would be for setting up a foreign jurisdiction over poetry, and making criticism a kind of Procrustes' bed of genius, where he might cut down imagination to matter-of-fact, regulate the passions according to reason, and translate the whole into logical diagrams and rhetorical declamation" (IV 176).

Hazlitt was heartened by later developments in Reynolds' *Discourses* which take a larger view of the genius of the artist and of his ability to stir response in a reader or viewer. In a brief but perceptive statement he provides a summary of Reynolds' critical career, especially of the critic's development from early traditional criticism to the more venturesome and imaginative spirit of the later work, the spirit which underlies his statement that genius in a traditionally lesser form of art is to be preferred to feebleness and insipidity in a greater form (VIII 122).

If Hazlitt operated within any tradition of criticism, it was the more personal, individualistic one inaugurated in large part by Wordsworth, although even here the attempt to categorize him is dangerous. His philosophical and critical roots were, to be sure, in British empirical psychology and in the complicated Anglo-Scottish aesthetics of the eighteenth century, with its emphasis on sensation, individual response, taste, genius, and a host of other ideas; yet everywhere he moved beyond a more strictly psychological orientation to develop a critical posture which was unique.

Hazlitt was the most personal of critics, eager to cut through the stultifying abstractions of rules, the maze of elaborate analysis, to provide open, unencumbered response. Indeed, for him, criticism becomes before all else the record of a sensitive man's encounter with a work of art. "I say what I think: I think what I feel" (V 175) almost typifies his credo. How to communicate that record with a minimum of academic jargon, of dilettantish pretentiousness, became the consistent struggle. How to find a language, direct or metaphorical, to convey the sense of the critic's sympathetic experience of the great work of art became the continuing challenge.

It was this personal, individual dimension which marked most of his critical writing, the sense that Hazlitt was articulating his own artistic temperament rather than associating himself with a particular school. He quite consciously separated himself from contemporary criticism and defined a new and higher ground as he contends that:

> A genuine criticism should, as I take it, reflect the colours, the light and shade, the soul and body of a work:—here we have nothing but its superficial plan and elevation, as if a poem were a piece of formal architecture. We are told something of the plot or fable, of the moral, and of the observance or violation of the three unities of time, place, and action; and perhaps a word or two is added on the dignity of the persons or the baldness of the style: but we no more know, after reading one of these complacent *tirades*, what the essence of the work is, what passion has been touched, or how skilfully, what tone and movement the author's mind imparts to his subject or receives from it, than if we had been reading a homily or a gazette. That is, we are left quite in the dark as to the feelings of pleasure or pain to be derived from the genius of the performance or the manner in which it appeals to the imagination . . . [VIII 217].

In his essay "On Genius and Common Sense" he expressed the essence of this conviction: "In art, in taste, in life, in speech, you decide from feeling, and not from reason; that is, from the impression of a number of things on the mind, which impression is true and well-founded, though you may not be able to analyse or account for it in the several particulars" (VIII 31).

Hazlitt took great pains to emphasize feeling and taste, not as mere subjective whimsies, but as informed and educated powers.

Mere enthusiasm is not enough to produce great criticism; it must, he contended, be tempered by reason and knowledge. Not everyone can conform to the new image of the critic. Only the "most refined understandings" (xviii 46) can operate successfully in matters of taste. Criticism as a profession has little room for democracy, for the tyranny of popular taste which stands to threaten the citadel of artistic excellence. Only "the opinion of the greatest number of well-informed minds" (xx 386) can become a true standard of taste.

The critic must be free of the tyranny of both past and present, must be open to all kinds of expression as he pursues his task with great catholicity of taste. Hence, Hazlitt ranged from Old English literature to Elizabethan drama to Renaissance painting to the works of his contemporaries. Prefacing his observations on Elizabethan literature, he says, "If I can do any thing to rescue some of these writers from hopeless obscurity, and to do them right, without prejudice to well-deserved reputation, I shall have succeeded in what I chiefly propose." He would "bring out their real beauties to the eager sight, 'draw the curtain of Time, and shew the picture of Genius,' restraining my own admiration within reasonable bounds!" (vi 176).

Veneration of the merely contemporary was, he felt, a major problem; too many critics have proceeded from the premiss that the post-Restoration years represent a literary Eden and have regarded all previous literature as Gothic, as lacking the elegance and sophistication of true art. Even where homage is paid to Old English literature, "it is more akin to the rites of superstition, than the worship of true religion" (vi 179).

At the same time he had little patience with the nostalgists, with those drawn to the art of the past as a bulwark of values they have inherited and now choose to set as standards, and uneasy with the new literature of complex emotion and imaginative complexity. Modern literature must be confronted, must be dealt with honestly and openly. "There is a change in the world, and we must conform to it" is his challenge. Critics cannot revive the spirit of Old English literature since they cannot push time backward; therefore "let us add the last polish and fine finish to the modern *Belles-Lettres*" (XVI 218).

Obviously, the demands on the new breed of critic are formidable, in terms not of acquired learning but of sensitivity, perceptiveness, and organic sympathy. No longer can art and criticism be seen as popular activities, as pleasant ways of expressing the deep and serious truths of reality. More and more, as Professor Park has contended and as we shall consider later, art was autonomous for Hazlitt, was self-authenticating.[1] It is an imaginative and symbolic re-creation of experience, valid in itself and having no obligation to point to some set of values beyond itself. Such a view of art demands a new kind of critic, a critic whose own work has the aura of art about it. "No man," he says, "can judge of poetry without possessing in some measure a poetical mind" (XVIII 182). Criticism, like art, is not progressive.

It is Hazlitt's image of the new critic, passionately intelligent, broadly informed, and richly sympathetic, which stands out so sharply in the early-nineteenth century. His task was nothing less than the justification of the arts and the sharing of their beauties with those readers and spectators for whom the arts are an intimate part of life itself.

NOTE

1. *Hazlitt and the Spirit of the Age*, p. 30.

4

Art and the Living Reality of Nature

> There is no language, no description that can strictly come up to the truth and force of reality: all we have to do is to guide our descriptions and conclusions by the reality.
>
> "On Reason and Imagination"
> [XII 45]

ALTHOUGH HAZLITT WAS a new kind of critic, not one who evaluated by pre-established rules of art or who operated with any pronounced sense of systematic procedure, there are, nevertheless, dominant themes or emphases which underlie his manner of dealing with a work of art. Most basic and most consistently utilized is the seemingly familiar critical commonplace that great literature imitates nature—and yet the view of nature seems dramatically new, associated, to be sure, with the more general Wordsworthian–Romantic vision of nature as a vast, living, and evolving process, but decidedly tempered and modified by Hazlitt's distinctive response to the new cosmology.

In Whitehead's striking words, "the nature-poetry of the romantic revival was a protest on behalf of the organic view of nature, and also a protest against the exclusion of value from the essence of matter of fact."[1] Throughout Hazlitt's critical writing is a persistent attempt to break through traditional abstractions of nature, particularly that dominant model of eighteenth-century thought discussed earlier, to see nature, not as the "one clear, unchanged, and universal light" of Pope, but as the concrete phenomena confronted in everyday life. "By nature," he contends, "we mean actually existing nature, or some one object to be found *in rerum naturâ*, not an idea of nature existing solely in the mind, got from an infinite number of different objects, but which was never yet embodied in an individual instance" (XVIII 150). In this sense nature is to be clearly distinguished from art and the artificial, from what he regards as those objects and emotions which are dependent upon the will of man and the arbitrary conventions of society. By "nature," he says elsewhere,

> and natural subjects, we mean those objects which exist in the universe at large, without, or in spite of, the interference of human power and contrivance, and those interests and affections which are not amenable to the human will. . . . We are masters of Art, Nature is our master; and it is to this greater power that we find working above, about, and within us, that the genius of poetry bows and offers up its highest homage [XIX 74].

Nature for Hazlitt has a naked, unconscious reality, an existence of her own to which art must render obeisance; she is the original, and art is but the copy. Hogarth's great secret in his pictures is fidelity to this image of nature. "Every feature, limb, figure, group, is instinct with life and motion. . . . What you see is the reverse of *still life*" (XVIII 161). It is the same with the magnificence of the Elgin marbles, which are "in their essence and their perfection casts from nature,—from fine nature, it is true, but from real, living, moving nature; from objects in nature, answering to an idea in the artist's mind, not from an idea in the artist's mind abstracted from all objects in nature" (XVIII 100).

In Hazlitt's sweeping view of the Elizabethan age, he often

reverted to this same premiss of nature. The writers of this period were, according to him, distinctively English, seeking truth and nature, not in external adornments, but in the honest and direct response of the individual to the world around him. With a spirit of independence and candor spawned by the Reformation, by the great translation of the Bible, by the exciting discovery of the New World, the face of nature was open to them, "and coming first, they gathered her fairest flowers to live for ever in their verse" (VI 191). For Hazlitt, Dekker, Marston, Chapman, Fletcher, Jonson, Middleton, Heywood, Webster, and Marlowe were worthy contemporaries of Shakespeare, true exemplars of the criterion of nature. "It is," as Hazlitt argued, "the reality of things present to their imaginations, that makes these writers so fine, so bold, and yet so true in what they describe. Nature lies open to them like a book, and was not to them 'invisible, or dimly seen' through a veil of words and filmy abstractions" (VI 212–213). Elizabethan tragedy was a very special manifestation, extending the scope of the design and intensifying the execution of ancient tragedy, and representing the essence of nature and passion free from the confining influence of a specific event in place and time. Shakespeare may strike us with his richness and power, and Sophocles with his simplicity and harmony. One is to the other as Westminster Abbey is to a Doric portico. Yet to set up either one as a standard of excellence is shortsighted and bigoted; it is "to deny the first principles of the human mind, and to war with nature" (VI 348). Decline has been the pattern since the Elizabethans as the dramatists of seventeenth-century France and England become increasingly preoccupied with the artificial and the rhetorical and set up barriers between the human heart and the freshness of nature. The French offered elaborate and vague dissertations on passion. The Germans presented characters acting not from the impulse of feeling, but as mere mouthpieces of ideas and speculations quite removed from the immediacy of real life. Dryden and English Restoration tragedians were essentially undramatic, exaggerating the commonplace and relying on extravagance of language and imagery to hide an essential lack of a sense of reality.

Restoration comedy was another matter, however, and Hazlitt found it difficult to award the palm unqualifiedly to Wycherley, Congreve, Vanbrugh, or Farquhar. Wycherley's characters, especially those of *The Country Wife*, are more natural than Congreve's. Vanbrugh "has more nature than art: what he does best, he does because he cannot help it. He has a masterly eye to the advantages which certain accidental situations of character present to him on the spot, and he executes the most difficult and rapid theatrical movements at a moment's warning" (VI 79).

Shakespeare was, of course, cited constantly as the great model of imitation of nature in Hazlitt's sense. He was not simply the copier in the mechanical sense; he was a co-worker with nature, a collaborator with her rich treasures and abundant variety. Eschewing any refinement or elaboration of the masterpiece, he remained open to her wondrous possibilities. If Chaucer, Spenser, Shakespeare, and Milton must be ranked as the premier English poets, then Shakespeare must be ranked as the greatest of these four precisely because he was "the poet of nature (in the largest sense of the term)" (V 46). The dominant characteristic of Chaucer's genius was intensity; of Spenser's, remoteness; of Milton's, elevation. Shakespeare embodied all these characteristics in abundance and went beyond them to express a unique greatness. Chaucer exhibited the vivid object in his work with a minimum of artificial drapery, and his faith in nature is at the root of his moving portraits of the grief and perseverance of Griselda, of the faith of Constance, and of the heroism of the child in *The Prioress' Tale*. Spenser possessed invention and fancy, qualities Hazlitt finds lacking in Chaucer, yet his love of romance, of the allegorical, sets him at a distance from nature. Milton was a poet of sublimity, of preternatural grandeur, the epic poet who provokes his reader to rise above mere nature to heroic kingdoms and larger-than-life characters.

Hazlitt's basis for relegating these poets to a position below Shakespeare's is interesting and yet true to his view that great art must at all times remain close to nature. "As poets," he argues, "and as great poets, imagination, that is, the power of feigning things according to nature, was common to them all: but the principle or moving power, to which this faculty was most subservient in Chaucer, was habit, or inveterate prejudice; in Spenser, novelty, and the love of the marvellous; in Shakespeare, it was the force of passion, combined with every variety of possible circumstances; and in Milton, only with the highest" (v 46). In a word, Shakespeare's love and devotion to the accurate and exact rendering of nature was central to his art; it served no other cause and thus accounts for the stirring reality of his plots, the sense of life as lived in his characters, the vitality and concreteness of his style. The tendency toward stereotype in Chaucer, the fascination with faery realms in Spenser, the sheer elevation and magnitude of Milton's artistic world—all these, in spite of their magnificence, have a pronounced tendency to draw the reader away from art's central responsibility to involve the reader directly and intimately in nature and life.

Metaphysical poets like Donne, Davies, Crashaw, and others are taken to task for ignoring nature as a subject and turning to the intricate, the remote, the far-fetched as a source of analogy. Such poets seek approbation, not for their subject, but for themselves, and hence they feel no qualms about straining probability. Donne's "Muse suffers continual pangs and throes. His thoughts are delivered by the Cæsarean operation." He and his colleagues

> seemed to think there was an irreconcileable opposition between genius, as well as grace, and nature; tried to do without, or else constantly to thwart her; left nothing to her outward "impress," or spontaneous impulses, but made a point of twisting and torturing almost every subject they took in hand, till they had fitted it to the mould of their

self-opinion and the previous fabrications of their own fancy, like those who pen acrostics in the shape of pyramids, and cut out trees into the shape of peacocks [VI 51].

Indeed poetry has undergone a steady decline from the time of Elizabeth to the present. Imagination gave way to the fancy of the age of Charles I and the wit of Charles II and Queen Anne, and degenerated finally into the poetry of the commonplace in the eighteenth century. Dryden and Pope were as great masters of the artificial as Chaucer, Spenser, Shakespeare, and Milton were of the natural. Hazlitt, echoing Joseph Warton's *Essay on the Genius and Writings of Pope*, does not dismiss Dryden, Pope, and other Neoclassic writers; he simply refuses to regard them as poets of the first order. Given the limitations of their world view, their concepts of poetry and the poet, and of the creative impulse itself, they achieved a remarkable degree of success. Theirs was an art of elegance and polish, an art more didactic and satiric, an art more concerned with "artificial life and manners," with "good sense and refined taste" (IX 239). Yet even among them there are priorities. Distinguishing very much as Johnson does in his *Life of Pope*, Hazlitt finds Dryden more natural than Pope, more uninhibited in his responses, more direct in his expression. Comparing the satiric portraits of each provides interesting clues to the dominant thrust of each writer's genius. "The difference between Pope's satirical portraits and Dryden's, appears to be this in good measure, that Dryden seems to grapple with his antagonists, and to describe real persons; Pope seems to refine upon them in his own mind, and to make them out just what he pleases, till they are not real characters, but the mere driveling effusions of his spleen and malice" (V 80).

Abstraction, any search for the type, the middle form, the refined idea apart from specific objects or circumstances, stands in marked and pale contrast to the density and fluidity of nature. From his early essay "On Abstract Ideas" he indicted it as an inadequate way of coming to know the truth. Sir Joshua Reynolds is frequently the object of his anti-abstractionism; he is "at the head of those who have maintained the supposition that nature (or the universe of things) was indeed the groundwork or foundation on which art rested; but that the superstructure rose above it, that it towered by degrees above the world of realities, and was suspended in the regions of thought alone . . . the glittering phantom that hovered round the head of the genuine artist . . ." (XVIII 150, 151). Truth and nature for Hazlitt were, not one, but many; not a monolithic unity, but variety and contrast and complexity within a living order. Abstraction is a limitation of the mind and cannot match the wondrous variety of nature, which is constantly yielding up new forms and new possibilities. It is not, however, abstraction or generality as such that he scorns, but rather the attempt to consider them in total isolation from specific and concrete manifestations. He favors "giving general appearances with individual details" (VIII 9). "We must," he contends, "improve our concrete experience of persons and things into the contemplation of general rules and principles; but without being grounded in individual facts and feelings, we shall end as we began, in ignorance" (XII 46).

Nature cannot be confined within certain boundaries created by the categorizing mind or epitomized in elaborate chains of being created by the fancy. Hazlitt revealed his eighteenth-century intellectual origins in his general Lockean suspicion of system-making and the particular distrust, so memorably articulated in such eighteenth-century works as Swift's *Gulliver's Travels*, Pope's *Dunciad*, and Johnson's *Rasselas*, of theorizing at the expense of reality. Experience was to him a vast phenomenon, embodying both the inner and the outer life, ultimately inexhaustible in its possibilities, and hence capable of providing new sources of understanding to those who achieved rapport with it and remained open to its rich gifts. Professor Baker describes Hazlitt as a pluralist "who thought nature so multiform and varied that it transcends not only our rules and categories and formulas but even our perceptive faculties. Anything we know, or think we know, is but an aspect of a whole that we can never comprehend."[2] For Hazlitt, natural objects and phenomena have a special kinship with the imagination and with poetry because they have a special identity and independence of their own, because, unlike the handiwork of men, they are generated spontaneously without tampering or interference.

Much of Hazlitt's most interesting speculation and much of his most vital practical criticism focus on the subject of variety and contrast within the unity of nature and on the consequent questions of how man deals with the variety and contrast and of how the artist represents or imitates them. Despite his ambivalent feelings about Coleridge, there is much of the latter's notion of the reconciliation of opposites, of multeity in unity, in his general approach to this problem. Nature is quite regularly seen as a panorama of contrasts. In his essay "On Reason and Imagination," he argues, "Any one thing is a better representative of its kind, than all the words and definitions in the world can be. The sum total is indeed different from the particulars; but it is not so easy to guess at any general result, without some previous induction of particulars and appeal to experience" (XII 51). Indeed, he contends elsewhere that one observation true in itself may contradict another equally true depending on the vantage point from which we view the subject. Even though Hazlitt himself was not a very successful painter, the whole subject and vocabulary of painting, as Professor Park has demonstrated,[3] plays a most significant part in his critical discussions of abstraction and concreteness in the work of art. In a discussion of one of his own paintings, he took issue with Reynolds' idea that minimizing individual details is an essential part of the perfection of art. With his own painting in mind, he writes of achieving "a gorgeous effect of light and shade," of making "the transition from a strong light to as dark a shade, preserving the masses, but gradually softening off the intermediate parts." Nature is once again the model for this rich sense of complication.

It was so in nature: the difficulty was to make it so in the copy. I tried, and failed again and again; I strove harder, and succeeded, as I thought. The wrinkles in Rembrandt were not hard lines; but broken and irregular. I saw the same appearance in nature, and strained every nerve to give it. If I could hit off this crumbling appearance, and insert the reflected light in the furrows of old age in half a morning, I did not think I had lost a day [VIII 9].

This idea of the reconciliation of opposites, of variety within an overall pattern of unity, is again manifested in human nature, which, for Hazlitt, was a continuing source of wonder and provided the artists with a fertile field of inquiry. He spoke with awe of "an infinity of motives, passions, and ideas, contained in that narrow compass, of which I know nothing, and in which I have no share. Each individual is a world to himself, governed by a thousand contradictory and wayward impulses. I can, therefore, make no inference from one individual to another; nor can my habitual sentiments, with respect to any individual, extend beyond himself to others" (V 101). Shakespeare almost perfectly captures this sense of the complexity of human motivation and the variety of human personality. His characters both in themselves and in their relationships with their dramatic peers are continually setting off contrasts in the imagination, continually sharpening the reader's or spectator's awareness of the complexity of experience. In a wonderfully seminal critique, he comments on a galaxy of Shakespearean characters from this viewpoint:

> For instance, the soul of Othello is hardly more distinct from that of Iago than that of Desdemona is shewn to be from Æmilia's; the ambition of Macbeth is as distinct from the ambition of Richard III. as it is from the meekness of Duncan; the real madness of Lear is as different from the feigned madness of Edgar as from the babbling of the fool; the contrast between wit and folly in Falstaff and Shallow is not more characteristic though more obvious than the gradations of folly, loquacious or reserved, in Shallow and Silence; and again, the

gallantry of Prince Henry is as little confounded with that of Hotspur as with the cowardice of Falstaff, or as the sensual and philosophic cowardice of the Knight is with the pitiful and cringing cowardice of Parolles [IV 293].

Borrowing from life itself, Shakespeare created characters representing a spectrum of human behavior, and he created them as a result of what Hazlitt described as an unconsciousness of imagination which matches the unconsciousness of nature itself. Such was the case also with the pictures of Hogarth, fluid, dynamic, exciting. Everything is in motion, and the genius of the painter was his ability to render the exact feeling of the moment, to capture the expression *"en passant,* in a state of progress or change, and, as it were, at the salient point" (IV 28).

So distinctive are Shakespeare's characters that actors play them at their peril; no other dramatist demands such subtlety of motivation and action. Hazlitt, like Lamb, was in large part responsible for the idea that the performance of Shakespeare in a theater must always be disappointing to an extent because the slightest departure from the vision conjured by the imagination is so immediately detected and so quickly a source of aesthetic displeasure. Hazlitt's criticism of characterization in the Troilus–Cressida story as told by Chaucer and Shakespeare is extremely interesting. Both writers dealt with the same cast of characters, yet each achieved a quite distinct artistic effect, an effect which he finds symptomatic of the basic direction of each. He finds no *"double entendre"* in Chaucer's characters; they are either serious or comic, and Chaucer seems too committed to them emotionally, too implicated in their affairs. Shakespeare, on the contrary, blends the serious and the comic, the straightforward and the ironical. According to Shakespeare " 'the web of our lives is of a mingled yarn, good and ill together.' His genius was dramatic, as Chaucer's was historical. He saw both sides of a question, the different views taken of it according to the different interests of the parties concerned, and he was at once an actor and spectator in the scene. If any thing, he is too various and flexible: too full of transitions, of glancing lights, of salient points" (IV 225). *King Lear* is Shakespeare's greatest play, revealing as it does the tension of the several elements of our being or, in Hazlitt's striking phrasing, "this firm faith in filial piety, and the giddy anarchy and whirling tumult of the thoughts at finding this prop failing it, the contrast between the fixed, immoveable basis of natural affection, and the rapid, irregular starts of imagination, suddenly wrenched from all its accustomed holds and resting-places in the soul" (IV 258). Macbeth's faltering virtue is nicely set off by the strength and resoluteness of his wife. At the same time, despite superficial similarities, Macbeth and Richard III are quite distinct, thanks to the sensitivity of Shakespeare to the complexity of character which they represent. Both characters are cruel and tyrannical despots, yet Richard seems constitutionally evil while Macbeth, a kind and generous man, is lured by accident, opportunity, prophecy, and a strong and persuasive wife to the commission of outrageous crimes. Similarly Hazlitt contrasts *Othello* and *Macbeth*, this time in a brilliant passage paying tribute to Shakespeare's ability to match "the profound workings of nature."

> The movement of the passion in Othello is exceedingly different from that of Macbeth. In Macbeth there is a violent struggle between opposite feelings, between ambition and the stings of conscience, almost from first to last: in Othello, the doubtful conflict between contrary passions, though dreadful, continues only for a short time, and the chief interest is excited by the alternate ascendancy of different passions, by the entire and unforeseen change from the fondest love and most unbounded confidence to the tortures of jealousy and the madness of hatred [IV 201].

Shakespearean comedy, unlike the artificial and the sentimental, offers characters natural and sincere. *Much Ado About Nothing* blends the ludicrous with the tender. Relying on rich contrast of personality, Shakespeare created in Hotspur and Prince Hal two of his most beautiful and dramatic characters. Avoiding the obvious dangers of stereotype and caricature, he made Falstaff not a mere sensualist but a richly comic character, old and fat, sensual and imaginative, with an hilarious disparity between his desires and his capacity for fulfilling them.

This strong anti-abstractionism is deeply rooted not only in positive critical evaluation, but also in specific approaches to writers and works which displease him. Overriding his admiration for the characters of the *Canterbury Tales* was his consistent reservation about Chaucer's tendency toward types of characters. Speaking of the pilgrims, he says that they "are every one samples of a kind; abstract definitions of a species" (v 24). They are, to be sure, distinct from one another but, unlike Shakespeare's characters, they are not varied enough in themselves. They lack the kind of artistic fertility which would enable them to yield up new shadings of meaning, new nuances of feeling. The root is in the narrative, as opposed to the dramatic, thrust of Chaucer's special talent. He tended to speak for and about the characters, and hence set up at least a partial barrier between art and nature. Again, Milton was not Shakespeare's equal, although Hazlitt's overall estimate was highly favorable. The criterion employed is similar to that discussed throughout this chapter. "Milton," he says, "took only a few simple principles of character, and raised them to the utmost conceivable grandeur, and refined them from every base alloy" (v 51). As a poet more epic than dramatic, he seemed not fully to trust the wealth of nature's resources, and consequently he sought to impose himself, to elevate, and to heighten.

Agreeing with Schlegel, Hazlitt contended that Ben Jonson's characters are more like "machines" than men, "governed by mere routine, or by the convenience of the poet, whose property they are." In reading Shakespeare "we are let into the minds of his characters, we see the play of their thoughts, how their humours flow and work: the author takes a range over nature"; in Ben

Jonson's plays the humor "stagnates and corrupts" or it is "directed only through certain artificial pipes and conduits, to answer a given purpose" (VI 39).

Hazlitt was especially harsh on his own contemporaries. Shelley indulged his love of power and novelty to such an extent that he lost touch with the flux of nature. His poetry was made "out of nothing"; good poetry may create "a world of its own; but it creates it out of existing materials." Shelley's poetry was "a passionate dream, a straining after impossibilities, a record of fond conjectures, a confused embodying of vague abstractions" (XVI 265). Coleridge's *Ancient Mariner* was his only genuinely successful poem. In a sense his art was ruined by German transcendentalism, by ingenious metaphysics, and he mistook scholastic abstraction for the ebb and flow of human passion in all its forms.

There was special praise in the realm of fiction for Cervantes, with the characters in *Don Quixote* communicating amazing variety and naturalism in themselves and in reference to others. The characters of Quixote and Sancho in particular are true originals, in the sense that nature has her own originals, "the one lean and tall, the other round and short; the one heroical and courteous, the other selfish and servile; the one full of high-flown fancies, the other a bag of proverbs; the one always starting some romantic scheme, the other trying to keep to the safe side of custom and tradition" (VI 109). Similarly, the characters, like nature herself, continually reveal wide-ranging complications of personality, obedient to those mysterious impulses which are deeply embedded in human beings. Their actions and manners are determined, not by the circumstances in which they are found, but out of their own uniqueness as it is touched and moved by the vicissitudes of human life. They "are so true to nature, and their operation so exactly described, that we not only recognise the fidelity of the representation, but recognise it with all the advantages of novelty superadded" (VI 110). Fielding was also a great novelist for Hazlitt, revealing the profoundest sensitivity to, and subtle observation of, the characters of men as he saw them actually existing. The richness of characterization in *Tom Jones* is unrivaled; and Abraham Adams is his greatest character, with the combination of truth to nature and a strong sense of the ideal. How much greater Cervantes and Fielding than Le Sage, who described manners instead of character; than Smollett, who seldom probed the wellsprings of human personality and consequently relied heavily on external situation and peculiarity of superficial appearance; than Richardson, who spun his web almost exclusively out of his own brain as if there were nothing else existing in the world. Hazlitt's comments on *Pamela* are vivid and again suggestive of how central a criterion nature was in his practical criticism. Arguing that no girl would write such letters in such circumstances, he advanced the notion that

> Richardson's nature is always the nature of sentiment and reflection, not of impulse or situation. He furnishes his characters, on every occasion, with the presence of mind of the author. He makes them act, not as they would from the impulse of the moment, but as they might upon reflection, and upon a careful review of every motive and circumstance in their situation. They regularly sit down to write letters: and if the business of life consisted in letter-writing, and was carried on by the post (like a Spanish game at chess), human nature would be what Richardson represents it [VI 119].

Hazlitt's vision of nature also eschewed didacticism and moralizing, any pained or artificial effort to point up moral patterns or lessons. Such a process he regarded as tampering with nature. There is, he consistently feels, a basic rightness in nature, a sense that she reveals her own meanings and mysteries, and that those who are truly unselfish and dedicated to her can detect them. Even the greatest artist, Shakespeare, was no more than a co-worker with nature, a humanized nature. "Art may be taught," he says, "because it is learnt: Nature can neither be taught nor learnt. The secrets of Art may be said to have a common or *pass* key to unlock them; the secrets of Nature have but one master-key—the heart" (v 355). Shakespeare, while seemingly the least moral of writers, was actually quite the opposite because of his complete rapport with experience, his complete commitment to translating its wondrous workings. He never followed the unfortunate and insipid path of romance writers who shun all mixed motivation and problems of complication in the interests of rendering life as they would like it to be. He had no patience with what Hazlitt regarded as popular and superficial concepts of morality which see life in terms of "antipathies." The pedantic moralist tries "to make the worst of every thing" while Shakespeare, whose "talent consisted in sympathy with human nature, in all its shapes, degrees, elevations, and depressions," tried "to make the best." Indeed, Hazlitt says, he would recommend Shakespeare as crucial reading for the Society for the Suppression of Vice (v 283).

The criterion of nature was, therefore, a strong underpinning in Hazlitt's literary theory and practical criticism, and yet he brought a unique and striking vitality to the familiar injunction that art must imitate nature. Impatient with the kind of idealism represented by philosophers from Plato to Kant, by the empiricism of Hobbes and Locke, and by what he regarded as the "middle form" philosophy of Sir Joshua Reynolds, he argued for a dynamic concept of nature as the arena of living experience, ever-changing and ever-evolving, the arena in which all generalization, all meaning, and all artistic beauty must find its source. The greatest artists, those consistently praised by Hazlitt, rendered their service to this nature. "He is the greatest artist, not who leaves the materials of nature behind him, but who carries them with him into the world of invention;—and the larger and more entire the masses in which he is able to apply them to his purpose, the stronger and more durable will his productions be" (XVIII 77). Such a statement could very well stand as Hazlitt's motto.

NOTES

1. Alfred North Whitehead, *Science and the Modern World* (New York: Macmillan, 1925), pp. 132–33.
2. *William Hazlitt*, p. 278.
3. *Hazlitt and the Spirit of the Age*, pp. 95–158.

5

Gusto and the Reasons of the Heart

> Why do we go to see tragedies in general? Why do we always read the accounts in the newspapers of dreadful fires and shocking murders, but for the same reason? Why do so many persons frequent executions and trials, or why do the lower classes almost universally take delight in barbarous sports and cruelty to animals, but because there is a natural tendency in the mind to strong excitement, a desire to have its faculties roused and stimulated to the utmost?
> "On Mr. Kean's Iago"
> [IV 15–16]

HAZLITT'S STRONG EMPHASIS on the centrality of nature in the artistic process is certainly not unique. Such a criterion is basic to a number of theories of art from the mimetic to the pragmatic to the "slice of life." What is distinctive is his special concern with the degree of engagement between the artist and nature and, subsequently, between the critic and the work of art. His are new questions and concerns: What is the posture of the artist vis-à-vis nature? What is the nature of the involvement? What does he bring to nature and what does nature bring to him, and what is the specific character of the new reality created by this interaction? What is the peculiar quality of the pleasure communicated by the poem, or play, or novel, or painting? Questions like these are persistently raised by Hazlitt, and the answers generally revolve in one way or another around the familiar, although much popularized and much misunderstood, concept of gusto.

This concern with gusto or emotional strength in a work of art is another cardinal tenet in Hazlitt's critical *modus operandi*. It is a highly psychological concern which once again suggests his debt to eighteenth-century aesthetic theory and distinguishes him from the more abstract and more philosophically minded Coleridge. He seems more interested in how art affects and less in how it is created; more interested in recording the quality of emotional excitement evoked, less in abstract theories of creativity.

As one moves through the great variety of his more general observations on literature, to say nothing of his practical criticism, it is remarkable to note the consistency with which the standard of gusto was utilized. He described the phenomenon in many colorful ways and in many different contexts, but there was one recurring emphasis. Gusto is "power or passion defining any object" (IV 77). It is "the conveying to the eye the impressions of the soul, or the other senses connected with the sense of sight, such as the different passions visible in the countenance, the romantic interest connected with scenes of nature, the character and feelings associated with different objects" (XVIII 106). Hardly an object lacks expression, a special and quite essential character, a close association with pleasure or pain, and "it is in giving this truth of character from the truth of feeling, whether in the highest or the lowest degree, but always in the highest degree of which the subject is capable, that gusto consists" (IV 77). In the fine art of painting gusto is "where the impression made on one sense excites by affinity those of another" (IV 78), the term here suggesting a totality of response involving the full range of human potential. It is, then, a strong emotional response triggered by the object in nature and brought to that object. W. J. Bate's description, "a strong excitement of the imagination by which, geared to its highest activity, it seizes and drains out the dynamic and living character of its object into telling expression,"[1] is perhaps the most perceptive attempt to come to terms with the entire process.

Gusto is absolutely central to the experience of art and criticism; it is ultimately what distinguishes art from a mere representation of reality, from what Hazlitt regarded as mere "objects of sight" (VIII 82). Only when these objects become the objects of taste and imagination, when they penetrate to the sense of beauty and pleasure in the human heart and are revealed to the view in their inner core and structure, does great art begin. One of his most famous definitions of poetry underlines his overriding preoccupation with emotional immediacy in his practical criticism. It is, he said, "the language of the imagination and the passions. It relates to whatever gives immediate pleasure or pain to the human mind. It comes home to the bosoms and businesses of men; for nothing but what so comes home to them in the most general and intelligible shape, can be a subject for poetry. Poetry is the universal language which the heart holds with nature and itself" (V 1).

Singularly absent in the definition just cited, as well as in his general association of gusto with great art, is the more classical ideal of decorum, of suitable subjects for the arts. As noted earlier, Hazlitt saw a fundamental rightness in nature and in the response to her workings, and he had little patience with the kind of moralism which views the artist and the critic as creators of moral patterns or as defenders of the sacred ground of an ideal nature against the incursions of the vicious and the ugly. The essential thing is that the artist be true to his response to nature and that the critic be true to his response to art. If nature is allowed to speak for herself, there is no need for a religious or moral arbiter to defend the cause of values. Nature is true, and art which records honestly our response to her presence is moral in the highest and fullest sense. In his important essay "On Poetry in General," he states quite categorically that poetry is "the most vivid form of expression that can be given to our conception of any thing, whether pleasurable or painful, mean or dignified, delightful or distressing. It is the perfect coincidence of the image and the words with the feeling we have, and of which we cannot get rid in any other way, that gives an instant 'satisfaction to the thought' " (v 7).

Hazlitt is extremely illuminating in his analyses of the place of emotion in human experience, and specifically in the formation of critical judgments. Here also is the strong psychological orientation, the preoccupation with human motivation, the suspicion of abstract theorizing. His credo is aptly summarized in his statement in "On Genius and Common Sense": "In art, in taste, in life, in speech, you decide from feeling, and not from reason; that is, from the impression of a number of things on the mind, which impression is true and well-founded, though you may not be able to analyse or account for it in the several particulars" (VIII 31). To rob a man of strong feeling, he contended, is to rob him of all that transcends the immediate objects of experience and the artificial ways in which men deal with them and to reduce him to an automaton. As already suggested, association is a vital part of the process, not the merely mechanical, automatic variety which he came to deplore in Hartley, but a much more subjective and emotional activity. For Hazlitt, nature does not operate in accordance with some preconceived rule of association; indeed, the workings of nature and of human response determine the rule.

> In a gesture you use, in a look you see, in a tone you hear, you judge of the expression, propriety, and meaning from habit, not from reason or rules; that is to say, from innumerable instances of like gestures, looks, and tones, in innumerable other circumstances, variously modified, which are too many and too refined to be all distinctly recollected, but which do not therefore operate the less powerfully upon the mind and eye of taste [VIII 31].

The genre of tragedy was frequently cited in Hazlitt's discussions of gusto. Once more he probed human motivation, and built a premiss which he confidently called "the common love of strong excitement." People are fascinated by and drawn to tragedy not simply out of a sense of escape or a preoccupation with the grotesque or abnormal. The explanation is quite the contrary: man's fascination with the tragic, his continuing desire to view the spectacles of Oedipus, Medea, Othello, Lear, and others is tied intimately to his basic humanity. Citing Burke's famous observation that although people flock to see a tragedy on stage, they would quickly leave the theater to view a public execution in the next street, Hazlitt went on to develop his own analysis. The explanation lies not simply in the differences between art and reality. Children still like ghost stories in journalistic form, and there are large audiences for the familiar, full, and true accounts of murder and robberies. The clergyman paints his dark and frightening canvas of hell much more often than he sketches an idyllic heaven. When we seek to discover why we would indulge our violent passions as soon as we read a description of those of others, Hazlitt pleaded succinctly that "we cannot help it. The sense of power is as strong a principle in the mind as the love of pleasure" (v 7).

Human beings yearn for excitement and love all those aspects of life and art which convey a rich sense of living things. And such exercise of the emotions is not necessarily harmful. Quite the contrary. If the vision of the artist is such that our sympathies are drawn to all the forms of imagination, good and evil, beauty and ugliness, hope and despair, exaltation and debasement, the effect is in the highest sense educative, formative, moral. Our experience is enriched and broadened, and much of the potential which is our heritage as human beings is tapped and realized. Strong passion represented dramatically in this fashion "lays bare and shews us the rich depths of the human soul: the whole of our existence, the sum total of our passions and pursuits, of that which we desire and that which we dread, is brought before us by contrast" (v 6).

Hazlitt was generally unhappy about post-Elizabethan tragedy, largely on the grounds discussed above. The plays of Moore and

Lillo are morbid and melodramatic; they "oppress and lie like a dead weight upon the mind, a load of misery which it is unable to throw off" (v 6). Dryden's plays, characterized by extravagant images, bombastic language, and a general exaggeration of the commonplace, are failures as tragedies. Addison's Cato is more a lifeless statue than a living man. As a matter of fact, Otway is the only Restoration writer who has produced a successful example of the genre, an example which rises above the ordinary to touch the human heart with its emotional strength. Contemporary German tragedy seems chiefly concerned with effect. Byron, a frequent *bête noire*, has turned tragedy into a vehicle for self-dramatization, a high-flown rhetorical drama in which the poet–hero pours forth his personal anguish for all to behold. Great tragedy, argued Hazlitt in the metaphorical manner which is such a hallmark of his critical writing, is "like a vessel making the voyage of life, and tossed about by the winds and waves of passion" while contemporary dramatists have converted it into "a handsomely-constructed steam-boat, that is moved by the sole expansive power of words" (XII 53). Instead of to a number of characters affected by particular and concrete incidents and speaking directly in response to them, audiences are treated to the spectacle of poet–heroes mounting a pulpit and delivering high-flown declamations on life, death, fate, and other great themes, all the while smothering nature with the virtuosity of their own rhetoric. What such drama offers are "the subtleties of the head, instead of the workings of the heart, and possible justifications instead of the actual motives of conduct" (XII 53). Rising to the level of principle, Hazlitt articulated the premiss which underlies such practical judgments. The trouble with such failures in the tragic genre is their intense and almost perverse preoccupation with the ego of the artist, and their consequent appeal to only one side of man's complex nature. More fundamentally, such plays manifest that ignorance of and indifference to that great cornerstone of gusto, its roots in the great world beyond the self and its magic ability to communicate strength of feeling as it is evoked by worthy and grand objects beyond the individual.

Shakespeare is the tragedian of gusto, and here Hazlitt challenges the Johnsonian notion that Shakespeare is more successful as a writer of comedy. His concern is not the analysis of some predominant or all-consuming passion; "it is passion modified by passion, by all the other feelings to which the individual is liable, and to which others are liable with him" (v 51). Again taking issue with Johnson's argument concerning the superiority of Shakespeare's comic genius, he contends that Shakespeare is the only tragic poet in the world in the highest sense, that Molière was a greater writer of comedy, that both Rabelais and Cervantes excel in such qualities as ludicrous description and the invention of comic character. Shakespeare, however, controls "the stronger passions," and the stronger the passions, the greater the work of art. His tragedies are "on a par with, and the same as Nature, in her greatest heights and depths of action and suffering. There is but one who durst walk within that mighty circle, treading the utmost bound of nature and passion, shewing us the dread abyss of woe in all its ghastly shapes and colours, and laying open all the faculties of the human soul to act, to think, and suffer, in direst extremities" (VI 30–31). The third act of *Othello* and the first three acts of *King Lear* are great exemplars of what Hazlitt regarded as the logic of passion. They

> contain the highest examples not only of the force of individual passion, but of its dramatic vicissitudes and striking effects arising from the different circumstances and characters of the person speaking. We see the ebb and flow of the feeling, its pauses and feverish starts, its impatience of opposition, its accumulating force when it has time to recollect itself, the manner in which it avails itself of every passing word or gesture, its haste to repel insinuation, the alternate contraction and dilatation of the soul, and all "the dazzling fence of controversy" in this mortal combat with poisoned weapons, aimed at the heart, where each wound is fatal [IV 259].

A problem play like *Measure for Measure* lacks gusto; the emotions seem at a standstill, and all our sympathies seem repulsed. *Macbeth* is a play in which lofty imagination triggers a tumultuously violent action, an action brought home to us with the vividness of our own experience. As in so many of Shakespeare's plays, the opening, with its wildness of setting, growing suspense, quick shifting of characters and actions, conveys a sense of absolute truth. The incredible designs of Iago, the dialogues in *King Lear* and *Macbeth*, the exchanges of Brutus and Cassius in *Julius Caesar*—these are still further examples of the dramatic fluctuation of passion which Hazlitt associated with gusto at its best. Marlowe, although a dramatist of great power, reveals "a lust of power in his writings, a hunger and thirst after unrighteousness, a glow of the imagination, unhallowed by any thing but its own energies" (VI 202). Beaumont and Fletcher begin the departure from the genuine tragedy of Shakespeare, thinking less of their subject and more of themselves. They lack gusto, for they lack that firm control of their subject and, consequently, are too often given to gimmickry and display.

It may be that for Hazlitt drama was the supreme exemplar of gusto and Shakespeare the practitioner *par excellence* of that genre, but his utilization of gusto was by no means limited to drama and dramatists. Gusto must be a vital effect of any successful work of art, the effect which must be experienced by critic and audience before any other criteria are brought to bear. It may reveal itself in the command of subject or grasp of character or intensity of expression, but its absence cannot be compensated for by mere form or moral or style. The poem, painting, or novel, like the drama, must engage its audience almost at once, must draw them into a vital relationship, must touch off a kind of emotional electricity. Milton, for example, "had as much of what is meant by *gusto* as any poet. He forms the most intense conceptions of things, and then embodies them by a single stroke of his pen" (IV 38). Although a more serious and sublime poet than Shakespeare or Chaucer, an artist whose essential genius was undramatic, he nevertheless possessed that strength of mind and vividness of conception which is at the root of gusto. His imagination "has the force of nature" (v 59). Satan is his great masterpiece whose "love of power and contempt for suffering are never once relaxed from the highest pitch of intensity," whose "thoughts burn like a hell within him" (v 64). It is in Satan and in the majestic account of the Edenic happiness and then the loss of it by Adam and Eve that *Paradise Lost* finds its greatest strength, and not in the battle of the angels or the rather stodgy dialogues in heaven. Milton takes his Biblical source and proceeds to describe its persons and objects with "the vividness of actual observation" (v 59). Not so *Comus*, which is without strong interest and passion. The great sonnet "On His Deceased Wife" reveals how the poet's mind elevated his thoughts through brilliant classical allusions and then enriched the allusions by the passionate involvement of actual thoughts and feelings.

Chaucer's gusto is different but no less effective. His descriptions of nature are pure examples of gusto, with "a local truth and freshness, which gives the very feeling of the air, the coolness or moisture of the ground. Inanimate objects are thus made to have a fellow-feeling in the interest of the story; and render back the sentiment of the speaker's mind" (v 27). More so than almost any other poet, he describes, not what his characters might be like, but what they actually felt, with all their impulses and prejudices. There is an absolute directness in his communication of the unique dimensions of his characters. "In depth of simple pathos, and intensity of conception," Hazlitt contends, "never swerving from his subject, I think no other writer comes near him, not even the Greek tragedians" (v 29). Compared with him, Spenser seems more remote from the vitality of life, interested more in beauty than in truth; consequently, his poetry lacks immediacy of feeling. His are the emotions of romance, "all that belongs to distant objects of terror, and uncertain, imaginary distress" (v 42). The inventiveness of his allegory is remarkable, but he has little comic talent and little subtlety of characterization.

Hazlitt had extraordinary praise for Edmund Burke among prose writers, a statesman who charges essentially non-poetical material with imaginative power and emotional intensity. In "Thoughts on the Present Discontents," "Reflections on the French Revolution," the "Regicide Peace," and other works, the full force of his genius is revealed. "He was completely carried away by his subject. He had no other object but to produce the strongest impression on his reader, by giving the truest, the most characteristic, the fullest, and most forcible descriptions of things, trusting to the power of his own mind to mould them into grace and beauty" (VII 309–310). His is not the set or formal style of Johnson, which

> selects a certain set of words to represent all ideas whatever, as the most dignified and elegant, and excludes all others as low and vulgar. The words are not fitted to the things, but the things to the words. Every thing is seen through a false medium. It is putting a mask on the face of nature, which may indeed hide some specks and blemishes, but takes away all beauty, delicacy, and variety [VII 310].

Hazlitt's observations on gusto in painting are both instructive and exciting. He praises highly the Italian masters, especially Raphael and Correggio, as "conveying to the eye the impressions of the soul" (XVIII 106). Titian's coloring is superb; his heads seem to think and his bodies feel. His flesh-color conveys the feeling of life, while Van Dyke's "wants gusto," since it has no "internal character," no "living principle in it" (IV 77). Rembrandt is a master; "everything in his pictures has a tangible character." Rubens is less successful, having "a great deal of gusto in his Fauns and Satyrs, and in all that expresses motion, but in nothing else." Raphael's "gusto was only in expression; he had no idea of the character of anything but the human form.... His trees are like sprigs of grass stuck in a book of botanical specimens." The landscapes of Claude Lorrain, "perfect as they are, want gusto.... They are perfect abstractions of the visible images of things; they speak the visible language of nature truly.... He saw the atmosphere, but he did not feel it." The kind of total absorption effected by works of great gusto is dramatically exemplified by the Greek statues where the "sense of perfect form nearly occupies the whole mind, and hardly suffers it to dwell on any other feeling" (IV 78, 79). While Michaelangelo's forms are full of gusto and "everywhere obtrude the sense of power upon the eye" (IV 78), Benjamin West, in his picture of *Christ Rejected*, "sees and feels nothing in the human face but bones and cartilages: or if he does avail himself of this flexible machinery, it is only by rule and method" (XVIII 33).

Gusto, then, a strong and passionate excitement in the artist which communicates itself to whatever object in nature it turns to, an emotional immediacy which pervades artistic subject and manner, form and expression, a psychological power which communicates the variety and complexity of human response, was a singular emphasis in the criticism of Hazlitt. Although it is important to emphasize again the relative absence of formal critical doctrines or regular procedures in the criticism, gusto is in a very real sense the answer to the question raised earlier. If nature is the multiformed, dynamic process envisioned by Hazlitt, how must the artist approach her and represent her? His answer seems clear: he must approach her with trust and openness and must communicate the life which is within her in the most vivid way possible.

NOTE

1. *Criticism*, p. 285.

6

The Higher Law:
Disinterestedness, Sympathy, Objectivity

> Egotism is an infirmity that perpetually grows upon a man, till at last he cannot bear to think of anything but himself, or even to suppose that others do.
> *Characteristics*
> [IX 224]

No sooner has the student of Hazlitt expounded on the significance of gusto or strong emotional excitement in his critical theory than he feels a strange sense of incompleteness, of not having told the whole story. For although it is quite clear that Hazlitt looked for strong passion in a work of art—indeed, that he was capable of great feeling and of shifting and violent moods in his own life—it is equally clear that he was almost always quick to cite and to condemn examples of extreme subjectivity, of what he often calls "sensibility," a "false and bastard kind of feeling" which is governed altogether by this reaction of pity on our own minds, and which instead of disproving only serves more strongly to distinguish the true" (II 230). Such sensibility is generally the result of a notable imbalance between the feeling expressed and that which evokes it, and, in Hazlitt's argument, is to be sharply distinguished from the gusto discussed in the previous chapter.

It is fair to say that Hazlitt never seriously qualified his demand for strong emotion in art. To him man's emotional nature is essential, and feeling is a vital dimension of the total psychic reality, a dimension which no system can ignore. Wellek is undoubtedly correct in associating Hazlitt with Wordsworth as inheritors of "the emotionalism and Rousseauism of the later 18th century."[1] And yet there are new understandings of this emotionalism, new modifications of the Rousseauistic commitment to feeling as a norm for life and literature. Professor Schneider is helpful in considering this new shading, suggesting that "with Rousseau feeling is always treated as a *value* in itself, an ultimate good, to be encouraged, increased, and indulged" while with Hazlitt "the value of feeling arises from its truth, that is, from the actuality of its existence."[2]

Hazlitt regarded emotion as essential to all the activities of life, and yet he so consistently underscored its dangers in his moral and critical writings that a pronounced theme emerges, a theme which is a hallmark of his approach to art. From his earliest years, long before he made any judgments on Shakespeare or Milton or Rousseau or Wordsworth, he had been most critical of theories, notably those of Hobbes, Condillac, and Helvetius, which portray man as essentially selfish. Of Helvétius' doctrine he contended that "to say that our attachment to others is in the exact ratio of our obligations to them, is contrary to all we know of human nature" (II 219). He sharply criticized Hobbes's principles, "That the sense of pleasure and pain is the sole spring of action, and self-interest the source of all our affections," and "That the mind acts from a mechanical or physical necessity, over which it has no controul, and consequently is not a moral or accountable agent" (II 144–145). Indeed, his early but major philosophical document, *An Essay on the Principles of Human Action* (1805), takes as its central theme the idea of the natural disinterestedness of the human mind and argues strongly for sympathy as the key source of human action. Man, so the argument goes, is most happy and most fully human when he goes out of himself and enters the "other" to share its living reality, its hopes, joys, and disappointments. Greatness in art, as in moral action, he says in one of his famous passages, involves losing the sense of our "personal identity in some object dearer to us than ourselves." In this context he is again in the tradition of Shaftesbury, Hutcheson, and so many of the Anglo-Scottish critic–moralist—aestheticians of the eighteenth century. As Professor Schneider contends, "For him the impossible is to be achieved not through assimilation of all *other* into the *self*, but through the projecting of *self* into all *other*."[3] Yet here again Hazlitt's idea of sympathy seems tougher and more muscular than that of his Shaftesburean forebears. True gusto, he contends, is turned outward toward a worthy object in nature, not inward upon the self. It does not dote upon itself or take comfort and pride in its own delicate nuances, but gathers its strength from the significance and power of its object in external nature. There must, he everywhere stated or implied, be a balance between the quality of the feeling and its source.

Egotism in all forms was his constant target. It is, he felt, "an infirmity that perpetually grows upon a man, till at last he cannot bear to think of anything but himself, or even to suppose that others do" (IX 224). Among many critiques of the egotism of his fellow-writers is one in which he charges Wordsworth with being

> jealous of all excellence but his own. He does not even like to share his reputation with his subject; for he would have it all proceed from his own power and originality of mind. . . . He tolerates only what he himself creates; he sympathizes only with what can enter into no competition with him, with "the bare trees and mountains bare, and grass in the green field." He sees nothing but himself and the universe. . . . His egotism is in some respects a madness; for he scorns even the admiration of himself, thinking it a presumption in any one to suppose that he has taste or sense enough to understand him [V 163].

Hazlitt is particularly interesting as he pushes his argument against self-centeredness to include even the so-called good-natured person. Good-nature, he states, citing Shaftesbury as an authority, is frequently a veneer for the most blatant selfishness among certain people. Such people, "as nothing annoys them but what touches their own interest, they never irritate themselves unnecessarily about what does not concern them, and seem to be made of the very milk of human kindness." Good-nature, as it is observed and described,

> is the most selfish of all the virtues: it is nine times out of ten mere indolence of disposition.... A person of this character feels no emotions of anger or detestation, if you tell him of the devastation of a province, or the massacre of the inhabitants of a town, or the enslaving of a people; but if his dinner is spoiled by a lump of soot falling down the chimney, he is thrown into the utmost confusion, and can hardly recover a decent command of his temper for the whole day [IV 100–101].

The breadth of implication for political and social action in this analysis is remarkable, and its indictment of the hypocrisy of the man who will do or say anything to avoid the unpleasant or the difficult rings with modernity.

There was, for Hazlitt, a great world beyond the ego, a world of people and objects and actions and conflicts, and this world must always take precedence over the petty hopes and anxieties of the individual. Even in the great world beyond there must be a sense of order, however strong responses may be, a recognition of priorities of all kinds. Simply stated, there is a scale of values. Some men are greater than others; some human actions are more significant and far-reaching in their effects and implications. Paradoxically, objectivity became the goal of the quest by the highly subjective Hazlitt: the greatest and most powerful human response is that evoked by what is great and grand in nature. He was quite straightforward in his contention that "besides custom, or the conformity of certain objects to others of the same general class, there is also a certain conformity of objects to themselves, a symmetry of parts, a principle of proportion, gradation, harmony (call it what you will), which makes certain things naturally pleasing or beautiful, and the want of it the contrary." Rejecting elaborate theoretical definitions of beauty, he relied on concrete examples "to shew that it is in some way inherent in the object, and that if custom is a second nature, there is another nature which ranks before it." Nor will the principle of association, so cherished by the empirical philosophers, explain this phenomenon. For him "the idea that all pleasure and pain depend on the association of ideas is manifestly absurd: there must be something in itself pleasurable or painful, before it could become possible for the feelings of pleasure or pain to be transferred by association from one object to another" (IV 68). Great works of art like Greek statues, the pictures of the Italian masters and those of the Dutch and Flemish schools, the caricatures of Hogarth "all stand unrivalled in the history of art; and they owe their pre-eminence and perfection to one and the same principle,—*the immediate imitation of nature*" (XVIII 111). Minimizing, as he so often did, expressionism, the idea that these masterpieces are "a voluntary fiction of the brain of the artist," he saw them as rooted "substantially in the forms from which they were copied, and by which the artist was surrounded" (XVIII 113).

Rousseau was a special object of Hazlitt's criticism. Despite a fine sensitivity, and the most delicate self-consciousness, he ranked as the supreme egotist.

> The only quality which he possessed in an eminent degree, which alone raised him above ordinary men, and which gave to his writings and opinions an influence greater, perhaps, than has been exerted by any individual in modern times, was extreme sensibility, or an acute and even morbid feeling of all that related to his own impressions, to the objects and events of his life. He had the most intense consciousness of his own existence. No object that had once made an impression on

him was ever after effaced. Every feeling in his mind became a passion. His craving after excitement was an appetite and a disease [IV 88–89].

In this temperament lay his special kind of genius, a genius which pioneered the modern sensibility, with its preoccupation with the personal, the autobiographical. Yet for Hazlitt this genius will always have notable limitations. Even Rousseau's fictitious characters "are modifications of his own being, reflections and shadows of himself" (IV 89). In almost everything he wrote, he "never once lost sight of himself. He was the same individual from first to last" (IV 92). Hazlitt drew fascinating parallels between Rousseau and Wordsworth as he plotted the course of the French philosopher's influence on the literature of his age. Both writers, he suggested, are incurably drawn to themselves and to all that they find important. "We conceive," he said,

> that Rousseau's exclamation, "*Ah, voila de la pervenche*," comes more home to the mind than Mr. Wordsworth's discovery of the linnet's nest "with five blue eggs," or than his address to the cuckoo, beautiful as we think it is; and we will confidently match the Citizen of Geneva's adventures on the Lake of Bienne against the Cumberland Poet's floating dreams on the Lake of Grasmere. Both create an interest out of nothing, or rather out of their own feelings; both weave numberless recollections into one sentiment; both wind their own being round whatever object occurs to them" [IV 92].

What Hazlitt observed and condemned in Rousseau and Wordsworth he regarded not as unique, but as a contemporary phenomenon of great social and literary consequence. He was most perceptive in his analysis of the new post–1789 thrust toward subjectivity in life and art, and provided, sometimes directly and sometimes by implication, a larger consideration of the modern temperament and of its evolution. The root of this thrust is closely tied to the liberation of self from the world beyond, the ordinary universe, and the extreme concentration on the individual psyche floating in a kind of vacuum and attentive only to its own stirrings. "The great fault of a modern school of poetry," he concluded,

> is, that it is an experiment to reduce poetry to a mere effusion of natural sensibility; or what is worse, to divest it both of imaginary splendour and human passion, to surround the meanest objects with the morbid feelings and devouring egotism of the writers' own minds. . . . To them the fall of gods or of great men is the same. They do not enter into the feeling. They cannot understand the terms [v 53].

Such writers, and among them Wordsworth and Coleridge are prime offenders, capture the spirit of the age, an age little concerned with objectivity as a value to be sought for in life and art, with the need for range and significance in the subject matter of poems, novels, dramas, or paintings.

While Wordsworth was part of a strong early–nineteenth-century reaction against the degeneration of poetry "into the most trite, insipid, and mechanical of all things, in the hands of the followers of Pope and the old French school of poetry," and while it took its basic inspiration from the "principles and events of the French revolution," a new individuality and originality brought with it dangerous results. Everything was to be natural and new; everyone did "that which was good in his own eyes" (v 161, 162). Wordsworth, as the head of the Lake school of poetry, was clearly an artist of marked originality, a poet of the inner life who reversed the critical priorities of a Pope or Johnson and made the expression of individual feeling central to the creative act. His best poems "open a finer and deeper vein of thought and feeling than any poet in modern times has done, or attempted" (v 156). In *The Excursion*, however, the image is buried by the sentiment. He "hardly ever avails himself of remarkable objects or situations, but, in general, rejects them as interfering with the workings of his own mind, as disturbing the smooth, deep, majestic current of his own feelings." He has no sense of objective priorities; "the great and the small are the same; the near and the remote; what appears, and what only is. . . . An intense intellectual egotism swallows up every thing" (IV 112, 113). So it is with the company Wordsworth introduces us to; there is no sense of rank, of importance, no sense that some men and women are more deserving of the attention and feeling bestowed on them. He was the greatest of nature poets, to be sure, yet however one may marvel at his rapport with meadow and stream, one cannot accept peddlers and plowmen as his heroes and as the interpreters of his feelings. Hazlitt rejected the idealization of rustic life. In his judgment "All country people hate each other." Not having been "accustomed to enjoyment, they become hardened and averse to it—stupid for want of thought—selfish for want of society. There is nothing good to be had in the country, or, if there is, they will not let you have it" (XIX 21–22).

More specifically, Wordsworth's great strength was the root of some of his most fundamental artistic problems. The magnificence of the poetry's internal power seems to exclude external form. "He has none of the pomp and decoration and scenic effect of poetry: no gorgeous palaces nor solemn temples awe the imagination: no cities rise with glistering spires and pinnacles adorned: we meet with no knights pricked forth on airy steeds: no hair-breadth scapes and perilous accidents by flood or field" (XIX 19). A supreme egotist, he sits in the center of his own being, ignoring the passions and pursuits of his fellow-humans and mining the treasures of thought and feeling lodged within. Unlike Sir Walter Scott, whose genius was external and took its roots in ancient ballad and song, Wordsworth was the genius of the interior life.

Lord Byron is a more extreme example of the egotism of the age, a writer who, for Hazlitt, existed, not by sympathy, but by antipathy. He wrote without a plan and has produced no artistic whole; his purpose seemed to be to stimulate himself and his readers with a momentary effect which will produce novelty and drive away what for him is the boredom of life. "He grapples with his subject, and moves, penetrates, and animates it by the electric force of his own feelings. . . . His *Childe Harold* contains a lofty and impassioned review of the great events of history, of the mighty objects left as wrecks of time, but he dwells chiefly on what is familiar to the mind of every schoolboy; has brought out few new traits of feeling or thought; and has done no more than justice to the reader's preconceptions by the sustained force and brilliancy of his style and imagery" (XI 72, 73). Byron's tragedies lack the essence of drama and never succeed in carrying the reader out of the recesses of the poet's mind into the scenes and events about which he writes. The heroes of his poems, whether Harold, the Giaour, or the Corsair, are all Byron himself, and the poems are the continual repetition of one subject. If a choice must be made, Hazlitt would rather be Scott than Byron. "We like a writer," he says, "who takes in (or is willing to take in) the range of half the universe in feeling, character, description, much better than we do one who obstinately and invariably shuts himself up in the Bastile of his own ruling passions" (XI 71).

Coleridge, another contemporary who cannot share the palm with his subject, has produced only one poem of real greatness, *The Rime of the Ancient Mariner*. A writer of extraordinary power, a mind of wondrous resources, he was always aiming to be greater than his subject and "has an incessant craving, as it were, to exalt every idea into a metaphor, to expand every sentiment into a lengthened mystery, voluminous and vast, confused and cloudy" (XII 15). *Christabel* is more like a dream than a reality, and the overall effect is obscure. "Kubla Khan" seems only a collection of nonsense verses. His prose style was turgid and affected; he sought to overdo everything.

Great artists continually manifest the virtues of selflessness, of faith in and respect for nature, for things and persons beyond themselves and their own needs and interests. They are outgoing; they identify and feel with their subjects and hence lessen the intimidations of individual whim and fancy. They find outlets and expression for their psychic powers in the broad scope of possibilities in the world outside themselves, and hence escape the fearful trap of egotism. Shakespeare and Milton, for example, "gave a more liberal interpretation both to nature and art. They did not do all they could to get rid of the one and the other, to fill up the dreary void with the Moods of their own Minds. They owe their power over the human mind to their having had a deeper sense than others of what was grand in the objects of nature, or affecting in the events of human life" (v 53). Shakespeare had no equal in this respect, not even the great Greek tragedians who seemed more circumscribed by Greek manners and sentiments while Shakespeare seemed to describe all the varieties of human experience.

Nature as a kaleidoscope of human possibilities was Shakespeare's focus; he was consistently disinterested and objective in his art. There was, says Hazlitt, a "generic quality" to his mind, so that it seemed to interact and communicate with all other minds and as a result gathered into its vast treasury a universe of thought and feeling. Such a treasury, with its incredible variety, made it impossible to develop any exclusive image of excellence or any fixed view of things. "He was just like any other man, but that he was like all other men. He was the least of an egotist that it was possible to be" (v 47). So great was his sense of the object beyond the self, so deep his capacity for sympathetic engagement, that he "had only to think of any thing in order to become that thing, with all the circumstances belonging to it" (v 48). At times he seemed to have no identity of his own, but to pass though every new variety of previously inexperienced being in his treasury, to be now Hamlet, now Othello, now King Lear, now Ariel.

Shakespeare's objectivity surpassed that of masters like Chaucer and Milton, certainly great artists by Hazlitt's standards. The predominance of the narrative element in Chaucer and the epic in Milton lessened the closeness of identification and the rich sense of the dramatic which lay at the core of Shakespeare's success. Great though *Paradise Lost, Paradise Regained,* and *Samson Agonistes* are, Milton's direction was basically epic in which "the imagination produces the passion" while in the dramatic "the passion produces the imagination." Instead of contemplating from a distance objects and characters grand and sublime, the dramatic poet draws his strength "from sympathy with the passions and pursuits of others" (IV 110). Brilliant though the tales of the Prioress, the Clerk, the Knight, and others are; vivid though the characterizations of the Monk, the Friar, the Wife of Bath, and others are, the need to create a fixed essence of character seemed to be primary. Chaucer's characters seem too much the children of the creator; "we get no new idea of them from first to last." Chaucer "told only as much of his story as he pleased, as was required for a particular purpose. He answered for his characters himself. In Shakespeare they are introduced upon the stage, are liable to be asked all sorts of questions, and are forced to answer for themselves" (V 50, 51).

If Shakespeare's gusto had its roots in his great sense of the natural, too many eighteenth-century writers lacked the quality because of their preoccupation with the artificial. Even though Dryden can be described as an artist of passion, he never went out of himself; he had strong sense and feeling, but his concern was not so much with what he felt as with what he should feel in certain situations. So also Johnson, a man of great learning and intellectual power, who "could not quit his hold of the common-place and mechanical, and apply the general rule to the particular exception, or shew how the nature of man was modified by the workings of passion, or the infinite fluctuations of thought and accident" (IV 175). One can praise the invention and fancy of Pope's *The Rape of the Lock* or the wit of *The Dunciad* or the descriptions of *Windsor Forest*; still Pope was of the second order of poets, and lacked those qualities of enthusiasm and imagination which the critic finds in great art. Though he was a critic, a wit, and a man of penetrating sense and observation, Pope lacked "a passionate sense of the beauties of nature, or a deep insight into the workings of the heart" (V 69); in short, he lacked the kind of sympathy which would have brought him to the innermost secrets of nature. In a very real way he became the standard of his age and set its tone and its ideals of poetry. "Instead of dazzling the reader with ecstasies, or startling him with chimeras, it now sought merely to embellish familiar objects, to laugh at petty follies, and to lend the charms of verse and the colours of the imagination to the commonest events" (XVI 156).

Great artists, on the other hand, continually reveal the virtue of selflessness, of faith in and respect for nature, for things and people beyond themselves. Unlike the Walter Savage Landor of the *Imaginary Conversations*, who seemed "bereft of voluntary power," and "the most wilful of mortals" (XIX 105), lacking openness to new ideas and possibilities, and unlike a James Thompson or a William Godwin whose work seems self-absorbed, Homer and Shakespeare and Milton were totally oriented toward the world beyond the ego. As mentioned above, the philosophical underpinning of these attitudes and judgments on egotism and objectivity was Hazlitt's youthful *Essay on the Principles of Human Action* written in 1805. In that document one can observe quite strikingly the evolution of a moral and, more important for our purpose, a critical, principle. There he argued that, contrary to Hobbes, the human mind is "naturally disinterested," that in a disinterested involvement with things outside of self one finds the basis of moral health and of an art of strength and significance. Far from being governed by pragmatic or utilitarian motives, man is naturally interested in the well-being of others in the same way as he is interested in his own good fortune. What draws us out of ourselves is something external found to be desirable; "there must be something in the nature of the objects themselves which of itself determines the mind to consider them as desirable or the contrary previously to any reference of them to ourselves" (I 18).

It is in this sense of projection, of widening the circumference of our sympathies to include the good and the evil, the noble and the ignoble in nature, and of representing this new range of sympathy with concreteness and vitality, that one sees the essence of Hazlitt's theory. It is as if, almost in Biblical fashion, he is speaking of the need to lose oneself in order to find oneself, to control and channel the subjective in order to express it fully and magnificently in art. A major remaining question, that of how sympathy is effected, of how the mind projects itself into the other, involves the major issue of imagination, for in Hazlitt the imagination, although many-faceted in its powers, is fundamentally the tool of sympathy, the link with the other, the magic passageway to the future and to whatever man wills as great and good.

NOTES

1. *History of Modern Criticism*, p. 190.
2. *Aesthetics of William Hazlitt*, pp. 36, 37.
3. Ibid., p. 39.

7

Imagination and the Ways of Genius

> We see the thing ourselves, and shew it to others as we feel it to exist, and as, in spite of ourselves, we are compelled to think of it. The imagination, by thus embodying and turning them to shape, gives an obvious relief to the indistinct and importunate cravings of the will.—We do not wish the thing to be so; but we wish it to appear such as it is. For knowledge is conscious power; and the mind is no longer, in this case, the dupe, though it may be the victim of vice or folly.
>
> "On Poetry in General"
> [v 8]

PARALLELING HAZLITT'S CONCERN with disinterestedness and sympathy as central values for the artist and the work of art is his elevation of the imagination as the power through which these values are achieved. One should stress the description of it as a power, since Hazlitt, like so many of his contemporary critics, was given to discussing imagination, not as a mere picture-making faculty or a compartment of the mind, but as a larger and more comprehensive capability which synthesized and unified the many resources of the human mind.

Hazlitt's debt to eighteenth-century British empiricism has, of course, been stressed. The scorn of abstraction, the emphasis on the primacy of experience in any theory of knowledge, the powers of association and coalescence— these are lifelong tenets of his critical credo. Yet, as he grew older, he rejected or modified the more mechanistic dimensions of the empirical tradition. Indeed, what is distinctive about Hazlitt is not only his peculiar approach to and modification of empirical theory, his use of experience as a foundation stone, but his addition of new and quite dramatic ideas on the mind's ability to mold and develop experience in accordance with its own desires and images. In Professor Albrecht's words, he "retains the mind's dependence on the senses but stresses its ability to deal creatively with the materials of sensation. As Hazlitt describes it, the mind can mold these materials into ideas and symbols, to which, through sympathetic identification, it gives objective truth and moral urgency."[1] Hazlitt, as he proceeded, revealed increasingly the impact of eighteenth-century Anglo-Scottish aesthetic theory. No longer is imagination regarded as a kind of variation of memory to be trusted only when its products are firmly anchored in a narrowly conceived reality. No longer is its value to be seen only in terms of its control by the judgment. One senses in Hazlitt's critical writing a liberation of imagination, an emphasis on its freedom to create and on its distinctive modes of operation, a consistent stress on its significance as a basis of moral conduct. He made the sharpest kind of distinction between reason and imagination. Reason, the remote, cold, and analytic power, is simply inadequate as a basis for moral or analytic judgment, and its inadequacy can be seen in three specific descriptions which he offers: "1. Abstract truth, as distinct from local impressions or individual partialities; 2. Calm, inflexible self-will, as distinct from passion; 3. Dry matter of fact or reality, as distinct from sentimentality or poetry" (XII 188). Imagination, the immediate, warm, and synthetic power, is triggered by strong feeling; "the warmth of passion is sure to kindle the light of imagination on the objects around it" (XII 46).

Imagination, then, is above all else a creative power, with that rare ability to shape its materials into a new reality which heightens our sense of the reality we see and hear. Strong passion triggers the imagination to seek and struggle for a mode of embodying the sometimes wild and indistinct cravings of the mind and will. The basic concern of imagination is, not with things as they are, but rather with things as they are touched by the peculiar electricity of our psychic lives. At times only the imagination, with its wondrous powers, can begin to match the infinitely varied responses evoked by the power of human passion; only the imagination can reveal a thing as it is felt to exist and as a human is compelled to think of it. In a quite brilliant passage, Hazlitt dramatizes the process as it relates to the imagination of the artist:

> Let an object be presented to the senses in a state of agitation and fear—and the imagination will magnify the object, and convert it into whatever is most proper to encourage the fear. It is the same in all other cases in which poetry speaks the language of the imagination. The language is not the less true to nature because it is false in point of fact; but so much the more true and natural, if it conveys the impression which the object under the influence of passion makes on the mind. We compare a man of gigantic stature to a tower; not that he is any thing like so large, but because the excess of his size, beyond what we are accustomed to expect, produces a greater feeling of magnitude and ponderous strength than an object of ten times the same dimensions. Things, in short, are equal in the imagination, which have the power of affecting the mind with an equal degree of terror, admiration, delight or love. When Lear calls upon the Heavens to avenge his cause, "for they are old like him," there is nothing extravagant or impious in this sublime identification of his age with theirs; for there is no other image which could do justice to the agonising sense of his wrongs and his despair! [XVI 63].

To the objection to Milton's *Lycidas* on the grounds that it combined Christian religion with the fictions of a heathen mythology,

Hazlitt replied strongly that although such a juxtaposition may seem grotesque to the limited power of the reason or understanding, to the imagination it is completely proper. Indeed, every classical scholar, even the most orthodox Christian, is at heart an honest heathen; the characters of pagan mythology have a reality beyond mere names, and it is this reality, with all its beauty and sublimity, which captures the imagination of Milton and other poets. Edmund Burke generally gave secondary attention to facts; "they were the playthings of his mind." To the man of great imagination "things that are probable are elevated into the rank of realities. To those who can reason on the essences of things, or who can invent according to nature, the experimental proof is of little value. This was the case with Burke" (VII 311). *Don Quixote* offers something "more stately, more romantic, and at the same time more real to the imagination than any other hero upon record" (VI 108). Apart from *Robinson Crusoe*, Defoe's fiction is too tied to fact and a narrow norm of realism which cramps the creativity of the imagination. Richardson's fiction, in spite of its artificial world, outdoes that of Fielding and Smollett in imagination. Although Fielding is a wonderfully natural observer of a great variety of human character, and Smollett a great caricaturist of eccentricity, Richardson is the imaginative novelist *par excellence*, creating, as he does in *Pamela*, a reality nowhere else to be met.

Among his contemporaries Wordsworth is a strong exemplar of the creative imagination who creates his own materials and whose poem *The Excursion* "paints the outgoings of his own heart, the shapings of his own fancy" (IV 112). Dividing poetry into two major classes, that of imagination and that of sentiment, Hazlitt described the poetry of imagination as "calling up images of the most pleasing or striking kind" and the poetry of sentiment as depending on the "strength of the interest which it excites in given objects" (XIX 18). The greatest poetry combines the best of both kinds of imagination, and Chaucer, Spenser, Shakespeare, and Milton exemplify them in the highest degree. Young and Cowley, dazzled by the ingenuity and exuberance of their own invention, lack quality of emotion. Wordsworth, possessed of extraordinary feeling, is

> deficient in fanciful invention: his writings exhibit all the internal power, without the external form of poetry. . . . Either from the predominant habit of his mind, not requiring the stimulus of outward impressions, or from the want of an imagination teeming with various forms, he takes the common everyday events and objects of Nature, or rather seeks those that are the most simple and barren of effect; but he adds to them a weight of interest from the resources of his own mind, which makes the most insignificant things serious and even formidable [XIX 19].

Walter Scott lacked this creative impulse, what Hazlitt called "this plastic power, this capacity of reacting on his first impressions." Whereas the true poet is "essentially a *maker*," Scott was a "learned, a literal, a *matter-of-fact* expounder of truth or fable" (XI 59–60). He was fundamentally an artist of the external whose strength was in large part in the richness of his materials, unlike Shakespeare whose great gift was in moving beyond the given materials to give them new life, new form, new meaning through the great creative powers of his imagination.

Imagination, then, is truly creative and has that rare ability to shape its materials into a new reality with a life and justification of its own. Again sounding like so many Anglo-Scottish theorists on the imagination's powers of coalescence and association and yet bringing to his own speculations a new vitality, he speaks of the imagination as an "exaggerating and exclusive faculty" above the demands of the logical and literal. In the interests of providing the sharpest focus and the greatest possible effect for an object of range and significance, it borrows from one thing to heighten another, it accumulates details and circumstances into a new unity. One is reminded of Keats's memorable phrase that the excellence of every art lies in its intensity by which all disagreeables evaporate, with essentials heightened and accidentals minimized. Reason or understanding, on the contrary, divides and measures, judging of things not in terms of their immediate effect on the mind, but according to their connections with one another. Whereas the imagination is basically a monopolizing power, willing to violate superficial ideals of equality and proportion in the interests of passionate intensity and realization, reason is distributive, weighing the relative merits of things in accordance with some abstract standard of ultimate good.

In its operations the imagination constantly associates, and its association transcends any merely mechanical process through a much more subjective association of objects and impressions. In defining the law of association, "as laid down by physiologists," as a process in which "any impression in a series can recal any other impression in that series without going through the whole in order: so that the mind drops the intermediate links, and passes on rapidly and by stealth to the more striking effects of pleasure or pain which have naturally taken the strongest hold of it" (VIII 35), he reveals his roots in the eighteenth-century associationist tradition extending from Hobbes to Hartley. In his much less mechanical and much more poetical analysis of the source for "our love of Nature as for all our habitual attachments" as the principle of association, he reveals his wariness about the limitations of empirical psychology and his own special need to bring the elements of human sensitivity and freedom to bear on a peculiar source of aesthetic pleasure. The setting sun, he argues, moves him deeply not so much from the beauty of the phenomenon itself as from its power to recall numberless thoughts and feelings which over the years have touched him deeply. "I remember," he recalls, "when I was abroad, the trees, and grass, and wet leaves, rustling in the walks of the Thuilleries, seemed to be as much English, to be as much the same trees and grass, that I had always been used to, as the sun shining over my head was the same sun which I saw in England." Yet he notes a difference when it comes to human beings. In the Tuileries

> the faces only were foreign to me. Whence comes this difference? It arises from our always imperceptibly connecting the idea of the individual with man, and only the idea of the class with natural objects. . . . The springs that move the human form, and make it friendly or adverse to me, lie hid within it. There is an infinity of motives, passions, and ideas, contained in that narrow compass, of which I know nothing, and in which I have no share" [v 101].

Imagination, which Hazlitt described as an intuitive perception of the hidden analogy of things, has an uncanny ability to penetrate to the core of a reality, to separate the essential from the nonessential, to determine when a thing is related intimately to a system or is only an exception to it. The "excesses committed by the victorious besiegers of a town," he reasoned, "do not attach to the nation committing them, but to the nature of that sort of warfare, and are common to both sides. They may be struck off the score of national prejudices. The cruelties exercised upon slaves, on the other hand, grow out of the relation between master and slave; and the mind intuitively revolts at them as such" (xii 51). Shakespeare's associative powers are enormous; his imagination is plastic and its movement rapid and circuitous. His images combine remoteness with telling familiarity; indeed, unlike many Metaphysical conceits, their fundamental truth to nature and closeness to human concerns seem a result of the ways in which unlike points of comparisons are yoked into a new kinship. Spenser, the poet of romance in *The Faerie Queene*, can evoke the mood of distant terror or imaginary distress; his descriptions, especially those of the Cave of Despair, the Cave of Mammon, or the change of Malbecco into Jealousy, assume "a character of vastness and sublimity seen through the same visionary medium, and blended with the appalling associations of preternatural agency" (v 42). Chaucer's special beauty lies in his intense concentration on and revelation of the essential in his characters of *The Canterbury Tales*. Although he touches on the many facets of personality in his creations, the overall impression is sharp and to the point. "The chain of his story is composed of a number of fine links, closely connected together, and rivetted by a single blow" (v 21).

The imagination's greatest power, however, is sympathy, its ability to project, to enter into another reality and to share its being. Again revealing a debt to eighteenth-century moral theorists, Hazlitt nevertheless goes beyond them in stressing the imagination's activity. Unlike memory and sensation, which are directed to the past and present, the imagination is future-oriented and free from the intimidations of past and present. Even the child, in pulling his hand from the fire or moving his lips to quench his thirst, reveals the futuristic or anticipatory thrust of the imagination "by means of which alone I can anticipate future objects, or be interested in them" and which can "carry me out of myself into the feelings of others by one and the same process by which I am thrown forward as it were into my future being, and interested in it" (I 1–2).

Hazlitt's practical criticism abounds in examples of the sympathetic and anticipatory imagination at work, but few are more suggestive than his treatment of *Romeo and Juliet*. His more general remarks about the play reveal, of course, a good deal of the enthusiastic response and the spirit of evocation which characterize his admiration of Shakespearean drama. "Nature," he says in describing his response to the play, "seems to put forth all its freshness; and the heart throbs with its full weight of joy, too soon changed to woe. The golden cup of pleasure, mantling to the brim, is dashed with bitterness: the intoxicating draught of youth, of hope, of love, drowning and ravishing the sense, is suddenly turned to poison" (IX 81). There is, however, as is so often the case in Hazlitt's approach to literature, a more systematic and analytic attempt to understand the special pleasure conveyed by the drama and its characters, and this attempt is very much rooted in Hazlitt's conception of the futuristic and anticipatory powers of the imagination. Shakespeare, he contends, cannot be understood in terms of Renaissance or indeed of eighteenth-century ideas of the role of imagination. As Hazlitt puts it, "Shakespear has but followed nature, which existed in his time, as well as now. The modern philosophy, which reduces the whole theory of the mind to habitual impressions, and leaves the natural impulses of passion and imagination out of the account, had not then been discovered; or if it had, would have been little calculated for the uses of poetry" (IV 250). Such a philosophy, and its inability to explain the intensity and magic of our earliest experiences, occasioned Wordsworth's Platonic answer to the problem of the *Immortality Ode*, an answer which Hazlitt deems unsatisfactory. "It is not from the knowledge of the past that first impressions of things derive their gloss and splendour, but from our ignorance of the future, which fills the void to come with the warmth of our desires, with our gayest hopes, and brightest fancies" (IV 250). It is this ignorance of the future and the anticipation which accompanies it which is so true to the nature of things and goes such a long way toward an understanding of the emotional states of Romeo and Juliet. Theirs are lives, not of reminiscence, but of vital anticipation kindled by the deeply sympathetic qualities of the imagination. Shakespeare, in Hazlitt's conception,

> has founded the passion of the two lovers not on the pleasures they had experienced, but on all the pleasures they had *not* experienced. All that was to come of life was theirs. At that untried source of promised happiness they slaked their thirst, and the first eager draught made them drunk with love and joy. . . . Desire has no limit but itself. Passion, the love and expectation of pleasure, is infinite, extravagant, inexhaustible, till experience comes to check and kill it [IV 249].

Romeo and Hamlet, although very different characters in many ways, are alike in the character of their imaginations. "Both are absent and self-involved, both live out of themselves in a world of imagination. Hamlet is abstracted from every thing; Romeo is abstracted from every thing but his love, and lost in it" (IV 254).

It is this conviction that "Desire and imagination are inmates of the human breast" (IV 250), that the sympathetic quality and futuristic orientation of the human imagination can be a source of great moral and aesthetic beauty, which serves as the fundamental premiss of Hazlitt's perceptive and memorable observations on *Romeo and Juliet*. Countless other Shakespearean examples can be cited. There is, of course, the memorable comment on the two major characters in *Antony and Cleopatra*, especially on the extraordinary sensitivity revealed in a single statement of Cleopatra's. Recalling her musings on Antony's thoughts and actions during their absence, Hazlitt remembers her " 'He's speaking now, or murmuring, where's my serpent of old Nile?' " and says: "How fine to make Cleopatra have this consciousness of her own character, and to make her feel that it is this for which Antony is in love with her!" The greatness of the line he attributes to an "intuitive power, the same faculty of bringing every object in nature, whether present or absent, before the mind's eye" (v 50).

The intensity of passion in *King Lear*, the speed of action and wildness of imagination in *Macbeth*, and the rapid shifts of feeling in *Othello*, all of which Hazlitt attributed to the breadth of Shakespearean sympathy, are exceeded only by the brilliance and perfect dramatic truth of Hamlet. Its hero is marked not so much by passion or will as by refinement of thought and feeling; the play forces no interest, leaving everything "to time and circumstances." The "events succeed each other as matters of course, the characters think, and speak and act just as they would do, if they were left to themselves." Such is the character of Shakespeare's imagination in these plays and in the creation of these characters. "His characters are real beings of flesh and blood; they speak like men, not like authors. One might suppose that he had stood by at the time, and had overheard what passed" (v 185).

Hotspur's rage when Henry IV forbids him to speak of Mortimer and his lack of sensitivity to all that his father and uncle do to assuage his feelings is a marvelous cameo to Hazlitt. It is, he says, as if Shakespeare made his imagination the handmaid of nature. "He appears to have been all the characters, and in all the situations he describes. It is as if either he had had all their feelings, or had lent them all his genius to express themselves" (IV 284). *Measure for Measure*, on the contrary, is less effective as a play because "there is in general a want of passion; the affections are at a stand; our sympathies are repulsed and defeated in all directions" (IV 345–346). *The Tempest* he regarded as one of Shakespeare's most original and perfect plays and the characters of Caliban and Ariel as examples of the magic of their creator's imagination. Caliban is an almost miraculous creation, "the essence of grossness, but there is not a particle of vulgarity in it"; the character's brutal mind is portrayed in contact with the original and pure forms of nature. "It seems almost to have been dug out of the ground, with a soul instinctively superadded to it answering to its wants and origin" (IV 239).

Hogarth's figures, Fielding's major characters, the Elizabethan dramatists—these and so many other examples underline Hazlitt's preoccupation with the imagination in its sympathetic dimension and his praise for it as a major root of the imagination's ability to create beauty which is truth and truth which is beauty. So often in reading Keats's letters, especially those in which he singles out Shakespeare for special praise because of his selflessness and impersonality, one hears sharp echoes of the great critic whose lectures Keats attended and whose critical posture he admired so much.

Imagination is the key manifestation of genius, another subject of great significance in Hazlitt's aesthetics and practical criticism. Indeed, in some ways the terms are practically synonymous. Such an attitude, of course, represents an almost complete change from the speculation which characterized much Neoclassic theory, and the change parallels in striking fashion the general shifting of critical priorities between 1660 and 1800. Hazlitt's speculations on the idea of genius were occasioned, to a great extent, by the rather familiar Neoclassic dichotomy between original genius and imitation, the chief spokesman of which was Sir Joshua Reynolds. Many Neoclassic critics, Dryden, Pope, and Johnson in particular, believed that it was not originality, but the acceptance and guidance of past models which produced the true work, and Pope's "Learn hence for ancient rules a just esteem / To copy Nature is to copy them" became a kind of motto. Reynolds, whose *Discourses* are an admirably representative example of eighteenth-century critical principles, had written quite decisively that "by imitation only, variety and even originality of invention is produced. I will go further! even genius, at least what is generally called so, is the child of imitation" because "genius cannot subsist on its own stock."[2]

Hazlitt in his essay "On Genius and Originality" opposed Reynolds' basic assumptions, arguing that any notion of connecting genius with accumulation of knowledge is seriously defective. For him it is "a power of original observation and invention," and "a work demonstrates genius exactly as it contains what is to be found no where else, or in proportion to what we add to the ideas of others from our own stores, and not to what we receive from them" (XVIII 64). It is, "for the most part, *some strong quality in the mind, answering to and bringing out some new and striking quality in nature*" (VIII 42). The essence of genius, then, is originality in the sense of totally new creation or of the fresh reshaping and recharging of the experience of others. Hazlitt set up a contrast between the Neoclassic ideal of reason or judgment and the emerging Romantic concept of genius, between spontaneity and naturalness on the one hand and correctness and artificiality on the other. To a great extent the man of genius acts unconsciously. He is not merely one with great intellectual capacity which needs development; capacity and genius are totally different, with the former relating to quantity of knowledge and the latter to the source and quality. With a typically Romantic emphasis on the subjective and original he contended that "A retentive memory, a clear understanding is capacity, but it is not genius. . . . There is no place for genius but in the indefinite and unknown. . . . He is a man of capacity who possesses considerable intellectual riches: he is a man of genius who finds out a vein of new ore" (VIII 46).

In no sense does the originality and exuberance associated with genius imply mere self-expression or, even worse, carelessness. Recognizing that the simple expression of individual feeling is easy and that much of the poetry of his contemporaries "is an experiment to reduce poetry to a mere effusion of natural sensibility" (XI 216), he grounded his idea of genius in "intense sympathy with some one beauty or distinguishing characteristic in nature" (VIII 49), and strongly held that "wherever there is true genius, there will be true labour, that is, the exertion of that genius in the field most proper for it" (XVIII 70). Nor is genius a progressive phenomenon as each age builds on the achievements of the past. Hazlitt took a particular and distinctive stand on the problem of the "burden of the past" and the "anxiety of influence" written about so perceptively and movingly in recent years by W. J. Bate and Harold Bloom.[3] Genius is not progressive, he argued, because it is not mechanical or definite or reducible to rule as science is. Genius loses more than it gains by transmission, and when the original inspiration has departed, "all the attempts to recal it are no better than the tricks of galvanism to restore the dead to life. The arts may be said to resemble Antæus in his struggle with Hercules, who was strangled when he was raised above the ground, and only revived and recovered his strength when he touched his mother earth" (IV 160).

Homer, Chaucer, Spenser, Shakespeare, Dante, Ariosto, Raphael, Titian, Michelangelo, Correggio, Cervantes, Boccaccio— these and other true geniuses lived at the dawn of their arts, and yet they generated them and brought them to magnificent levels of perfection. They were not, as much Neoclassic criticism dealt with them, diamonds in the rough, untutored and formless geniuses who manifest wit without judgment, beauty without art. Milton, almost alone among artists of later ages, seems to belong in their company. There have been great artists in the later ages of polish and cultivation—Hazlitt cites Tasso and Pope, Guido and Vandyke—but they were inferior to the almost divine originality and massive strength and vision of the great pioneers.

In a very real sense Hazlitt's brilliant conception of the creative and sympathetic imagination, his dynamic concept of genius, his persistent quest for originality were key features of the growing Romantic critical spirit of his time. If man's emotions are good and trustworthy when rooted in the grand and worthy objects of nature, the ideal course to follow was to express these emotions through the imagination's power to find their analogues in nature. The man of real genius "has the feeling of truth already shrined in his own breast, and his eye is still bent on nature to see how she expresses herself" (VIII 41). Therefore, he argued, the poet of genius should pay less attention to rules, traditions, and customs, and look into his own heart and write. Insofar as the poet does this, his art gains originality and uniqueness, and with Hazlitt, as with a growing number of early–nineteenth-century critics, these values increasingly became the focus of literary criticism.

NOTES

1. *Hazlitt and the Creative Imagination*, p. 2.
2. Ed. Helen Zimmern (London: Scott, 1887), pp. 77, 81.
3. Bate, *Burden of the Past*; Harold Bloom, *The Anxiety of Influence: A Theory of Poetry* (New York: Oxford University Press, 1973).

8

Literature, Criticism, and the New Manifesto

> If poetry is a dream, the business of life is much the same. If it is a fiction, made up of what we wish things to be, and fancy that they are, because we wish them so, there is no other nor better reality. Ariosto has described the loves of Angelica and Medoro: but was not Medoro, who carved the name of his mistress on the barks of trees, as much enamoured of her charms as he? Homer has celebrated the anger of Achilles: but was not the hero as mad as the poet? Plato banished the poets from his Commonwealth, lest their descriptions of the natural man should spoil his mathematical man, who was to be without passions and affections, who was neither to laugh nor weep, to feel sorrow nor anger, to be cast down nor elated by any thing. This was a chimera, however, which never existed but in the brain of the inventor; and Homer's poetical world has outlived Plato's philosophical Republic.
>
> "On Poetry in General"
> [v 3]

OVERRIDING ALL THE SPECIAL EMPHASES and techniques of Hazlitt's practice as a critic and theorist is what may be described as a new implicit and explicit manifesto for poetry and indeed for the arts in general. The deepest themes of the manifesto, the uniqueness and autonomy of poetry and its power to represent reality in fresh and original ways, were, of course, articulated by contemporaries like Wordsworth and Shelley, but Hazlitt's distinctive formulation stands as a major contribution to the development of aesthetics and criticism in the nineteenth century.[1] Professor Park, who so perceptively traces the struggle of poetry to liberate itself from the intimidations of scientific abstraction in the early-nineteenth century and to take up the cause of philosophy and theology, succinctly describes the problem confronted by Hazlitt as "whether poetry is poetry, or whether it is finally explicable only within the framework of a more general metaphysic."[2]

Students of the problem are, of course, familiar with Wordsworth's memorable attempt in the Preface to the Second Edition of the *Lyrical Ballads* (1800) to assert the uniqueness of poetry and the ability to express those deeper and more spiritual truths which transcend the world of fact and particularity to which science addresses itself. Poetry for Wordsworth does not exist to serve the cause of science or philosophy or history; indeed, it is greater than all these in its wondrous power to move beyond the limitations which impede their progress and to express the mysterious and the intangible. Poetry's object, he says, and he echoes Aristotle's answer to Plato, is "truth, not individual and local, but general, and operative; not standing upon external testimony, but carried alive into the heart by passion; truth which is its own testimony, which gives competence and confidence to the tribunal to which it appeals, and receives them from the same tribunal." Poetry, with its own special goals and methodology, is greater than science; for its mode of dealing with truth is to render it immediate and realizable to the human heart, while science, no less concerned with truth, nevertheless deals with it in more detached and dispassionate ways. Though both poet and man of science share a pleasure in knowledge, "the knowledge of the one cleaves to us as a necessary part of our existence, our natural and unalienable inheritance; the other is a personal and individual acquisition, slow to come to us, and by no habitual and direct sympathy connecting us with our fellow-beings."[3]

Shelley also shares the Wordsworthian and the general Romantic preoccupation with new questions at the beginning of the nineteenth century: What is poetry in its essence? Is it simply a more pleasant form of expressing the truths of philosophy and theology? Is its metaphorical and symbolic mode simply an adornment of the deeper truths of hard knowledge? Although a more exuberant document than Wordsworth's Preface, Shelley's *A Defence of Poetry* is no less unqualified and confident in its critique of reason and didacticism and its defense of poetry as a form of inspired knowledge which must become the source of man's salvation in an increasingly materialistic world. The document rings with oft-quoted phrases and sentences attesting to the new theme of the autonomy of poetry. "Poetry" for him is " 'the expression of the imagination': and poetry is connate with the origin of man." The poet "participates in the eternal, the infinite, and the one; as far as relates to his conceptions, time and place and number are not," and poets as a class are "the unacknowledged legislators of the world." With an extraordinary concern for the ethical dimension of poetry, he argues that the "great instrument of moral good is the imagination; and poetry administers to the effect by acting upon the cause. Poetry enlarges the circumference of the imagination by replenishing it with thoughts of ever new delight, which have the power of attracting and assimilating to their own nature all other thoughts, and which form new intervals and interstices whose void for ever craves fresh food."[4]

The new mission of poetry is clearly set at the beginning of the nineteenth century, then, and Hazlitt, although less evangelical in his mode of expression, is no less urgent in his need to talk about the mission and its implications not just for specific writings, but for criticism and for life itself. Although the new critic is a man of strong feeling interested in describing his response to the work of art, and although criticism is the record of an emotional encounter rather than a process of clinical analysis of texts and application of pre-established rules, some of Hazlitt's most urgent questions revolve around the meaning of poetry itself. He seems consistently interested in poetry's deepest roots, its connections with life, the peculiar mode by which it represents life, and the special character of its impact on human personality. Too often the reader remembers the more superficial and glamorous manner by which Hazlitt uses metaphor or evocation to express a critical response and misses the deeper thrust of a critical methodology which takes him to the very basic questions suggested above. Hazlitt does have a quite amazing capacity, in spite of his gospel of gusto, to stand back from the particulars of the act of criticism and to isolate the larger and essential issues which are ultimately grounded in aesthetics.

Poetry—and literature in general—is intimately related to life and to human life in particular, and, in spite of its personal and passionate thrust, is a vision of life, not just a mode for revealing the personal ingenuity or self-expression of the artist. Quite the contrary, it seeks to minimize personality to such an extent that the artist is able to draw the work into the most intimate kind of imitation of its object. The world of fact, of didacticism, and of personality must be remote for the poet who would truly capture the essential reality which surrounds him.

Like his contemporaries, Hazlitt begins with the presumption that poetry is no ordinary gift, no merely elegant form of dealing with the everyday. Citing Bacon as his authority, he sees poetry as having something of the divine in it, something which renders it unique instead of ancillary to rhetoric or philosophy or theology. It is, he says,

> strictly the language of the imagination; and the imagination is that faculty which represents objects, not as they are in themselves, but as they are moulded by other thoughts and feelings, into an infinite variety of shapes and combinations of power. This language is not the

less true to nature, because it is false in point of fact; but so much the more true and natural, if it conveys the impression which the object under the influence of passion makes on the mind [v 4].

Unlike history, which "treats, for the most part, of the cumbrous and unwieldly masses of things, the empty cases in which the affairs of the world are packed" (v 2), poetry, taking its cue from Terence, is dedicated to the principle that nothing human can be foreign to it. It is not "a branch of authorship: it is 'the stuff of which our life is made'" (v 2). It moves beyond the mere recital of objects and facts, the mere delineation of natural feelings; indeed it becomes true poetry only when the heightening power of imagination charges objects, facts, and feelings with a new and powerful life. Poetry of this kind becomes the most emphatic of all languages, a language which symbolically translates those yearnings and desires of the human mind which make man essentially what he is and poetry such a vital part of life for both artist and audience.

Not only is poetry the language of imagination and passion and not only does it draw its sustenance from life; it is addressed to life and achieves its unique effects only as it touches human beings in vital ways. Not a mere source of escape and entertainment or a vehicle for instructive platitudes, it is a vision of the essential dimension of experience; it is purposeful in the best sense. It "comes home to the bosoms and businesses of men; for nothing but what so comes home to them in the most general and intelligible shape, can be a subject for poetry" (v 1). Poetry's ability to capture truth imaginatively and to render it vivid to the human spirit is truly a formative process by which experience is nourished and broadened, a process which is educative in the richest sense of the word. Hazlitt stressed how central this process is to poetry on many occasions, notably when he argued that poetry can be detected "wherever a movement of imagination or passion is impressed on the mind, by which it seeks to prolong and repeat the emotion, to bring all other objects into accord with it, and to give the same movement of harmony, sustained and continuous, or gradually varied according to the occasion" (v 12).

Certainly no genre is more exemplary of literature's moral force than tragedy, which was the model of Hazlitt's earlier discussed criterion of sympathy or disinterestedness. By providing the spectacle of the great man confronting his essential limitedness, it replaces mere selfishness with imaginary sympathy and gives us an interest and involvement in humanity itself, evoking those intellectual, imaginative, and emotional facets of human response which make man essentially what he is. Hazlitt's metaphor is an apt one: tragedy "opens the chambers of the human heart. It leaves nothing indifferent to us that can affect our common nature" (IV 200). Again he speaks of tragedy as the most impassioned poetry and traces its moral force with brilliant imagery: tragedy

> strives to carry on the feeling to the utmost point of sublimity or pathos, by all the force of comparison or contrast; loses the sense of present suffering in the imaginary exaggeration of it; exhausts the terror or pity by an unlimited indulgence of it; grapples with impossibilities in its desperate impatience of restraint; throws us back upon the past, forward into the future; brings every moment of our being or object of nature in startling review before us; and in the rapid whirl of events, lifts us from the depths of woe to the highest contemplations on human life [v 5].

In a survey of poetry in the world, he saw only decline, from Homer's brilliant sense of life and action to a certain abstractness in the Bible, to a personification of blind will in Dante, to the decay of life and the sense of privation in Ossian.

The examples could be multiplied, but they would add little to a point already strikingly clear: namely, Hazlitt's critical preoccupation with poetry as a unique form of representing what is essential in experience, its reliance on the symbolic language of the imagination to penetrate the human heart and to open it up to the rich and wondrous possibilities of human life and character. This truly moral dimension was always his first concern and was the occasion for many of his most searching observations on how the morality of art renders futile the rather strident demands that art be more didactic and more overtly instructive in its method. He continually stressed that the most moral writers do not pretend to inculcate any moral and that overt preaching in art weakens that art irreparably. The great English novelists, for example, vividly capture human manners and leave the audience to draw the inferences. The writer of comedy ought simply "to open the volume of nature and the world for his living materials, and not take them out of his ethical common-place book" (VI 157). Drama, without ever becoming preachy or moralistic, can epitomize Hazlitt's belief that good and evil are not fictions but realities in a real world, and that by giving itself freely to nature,

> it is its own voucher for the truth of the inferences it draws, for its warnings, or its examples; that it brings out the higher, as well as lower principles of action, in the most striking and convincing points of view; satisfies us that virtue is not a mere shadow; clothes it with passion, imagination, reality, and, if I may so say, translates morality from the language of theory into that of practice [VI 157].

Hazlitt turned to all kinds of literature to illustrate his belief in the moral force of art. He was touched by the garden scene at Shallow's country seat in Shakespeare's *Henry IV*, by the dialogue between Shallow and Silence on the death of old Double with its happy combination of wisdom and foolishness. The scenes are superior for him because they draw from "the stuff we are made of" and deeply affect us by their stunning revelation of *"what a little thing is human life,* what a poor forked creature man is!" (IV 283). *Coriolanus*, with its dramatic moral that the poor and humble will be made poorer and the great will further strengthen themselves at the expense of others, reveals "the logic of the imagination and the passions; which seek to aggrandize what excites admiration, and to heap contempt on misery," and he concludes that "what men delight to read in books, they will put in practice in reality" (v 349, 350). *King Lear* is almost the perfect play because it reminds us how closely poetry touches the most interesting aspects of life and further illustrates that the man with a contempt for poetry is a man with a contempt for himself and humanity. It clarifies the essential superiority of poetry to painting since our strongest memories relate to emotions and not to faces. But, above all—and here Hazlitt seems to be at his psychological and critical best in describing the moral effect of the play—it actually engages the full range of the human spirit. In lines which again clearly seem to anticipate Keats's "the excellence of every Art is its intensity, capable of making all disagreeables evaporate, from their being in close relationship with Beauty and Truth—Examine 'King Lear,' & you will find this exemplified throughout,"[5] he proceeds to examine the special ways in which the play engages us. What makes great tragedy bearable and constructive for us is a certain balance of pleasure and pain so that "in proportion to the greatness of the evil, is our sense and desire of the opposite good excited," and "our sympathy with actual suffering is lost in the strong impulse given to our natural affections, and carried away with the swelling tide of passion, that gushes from and relieves the heart" (iv 272). Shakespeare's lack of overt religious enthusiasm or moral concern stands apart from the strong religious zeal which is so much a part of Milton's poetry. Milton was never indifferent as an artist and would never take as much delight in conceiving an Iago as an Imogen. He wrote with the ideals of the Hebrew theocracy and the perfect Commonwealth as fixed points of his sensibility, "with a hand just warm from the touch of the ark of faith." His sympathetic powers were always secondary to his larger purposes; his "religious zeal infused its character into his imagination; so that he devotes himself with the same sense of duty to the cultivation of his genius, as he did to the exercise of virtue, or the good of his country" (v 56–57). As with Shakespeare and Milton, so also with lesser lights like Sheridan and Steele. Although the comedies of Steele were written not to imitate life but to reform the morals of the age, Sheridan, especially in an almost perfect comedy like *The School for Scandal*, uses the firm but light touch to carry on his satire. Hazlitt notes that "every thing in them *tells*; there is no labour in vain." The spirit of *The School for Scandal* is, not preachy, but open and generous. It seems unaffected by the moralistic strictures of Jeremy Collier and reveals a generosity and openness "that relieves the heart as well as clears the lungs" (VI 165).

Despite Hazlitt's deep commitment to the autonomy and self-authenticating character of poetry, to poetry's ability to teach imaginatively and emotionally, he sensed a twofold decline. The Neoclassic preoccupation with art as a vehicle for rather direct moral instruction and the contemporary concern with art as self-revelation have taken a serious toll. He saw his own time as critical, didactic, paradoxical, and romantic in the bad sense of the term; it lacked the essentially dramatic quality which great art requires, and consequently no great comedies and tragedies were being written. The French Revolution is obviously a major source of the problem as Englishmen have become a nation of newsmongers and politicians. They have become public creatures, arguing national questions, the rise of stocks, the fighting of battles, the fate of kingdoms.

> We participate in the general progress of intellect, and the large vicissitudes of human affairs; but the hugest private sorrow looks dwarfish and puerile. In the sovereignty of our minds, we make mankind our quarry; and, in the scope of our ambitious thoughts, hunt for prey through the four quarters of the world. In a word, literature and civilization have abstracted man from himself so far, that his existence is no longer *dramatic*; and the press has been the ruin of the stage, unless we are greatly deceived [XVIII 305].

Yet the roots go even deeper, and, in a manner which reminds us of Wordsworth's complaints in the Preface to the *Lyrical Ballads*, Hazlitt speaks of the problem of the audience of poetry itself, a loss of taste and of the ability to respond with the full range of human sensibility. Like Wordsworth, he believes that although artists may still be intimidated by a certain traditionalism and a sense of the burden of past greatness, there is an equally serious problem in the state of public taste. Wordsworth spoke of the great national events and the increasing accumulation of men in cities as contributing factors to the blunting of the sensibilities of the audience for poetry. Hazlitt, deeply convinced that "no single mind can move in direct opposition to the vast machine of the world around it" and that the "public taste hangs like a millstone round the neck of all original genius that does not conform to established and exclusive models" (v 96), finds no sympathy for the artist who would cut a deeper vein of feeling, who would confront audiences with their deepest selves through the symbolic and charged language of poetry. Something basic has been lost, the capacity to imagine greatly, to feel freely and passionately, to involve the self in the great objects of nature, to believe in myth as a conduit of the mysteries of the universe. Hazlitt argues that there can never be another Jacob's dream unless a revolution in taste is effected, unless artists and audiences recapture the primitive sense of wonder. The heavens have gone farther away as the increase of knowledge and the quite necessary development and refinement of civilization have challenged the province of poetry and constructed mechanisms which lead us safely but insipidly from cradle to grave.

> The heroes of the fabulous ages rid the world of monsters and giants. At present we are less exposed to the vicissitudes of good or evil, to the incursions of wild beasts or "bandit fierce," or to the unmitigated fury of the elements.... But the police spoils all; and we now hardly so much as dream of a midnight murder. Macbeth is only tolerated in this country for the sake of the music; and in the United States of America, where the philosophical principles of government are carried still

further in theory and practice, we find the Beggar's Opera is hooted from the stage [v 9–10].

And yet Hazlitt, like Wordsworth and Shelley, refused to despair over the contemporary scene. Indeed he spoke and wrote with even greater urgency about the mission of literature and the arts in such a world, about their power to renovate the sensibility and to create a new freshness and readiness of response. In a larger sense he positioned literature at the heart of any system, formal or informal, of liberal education, the only kind of education which can educe the richest possibilities of man's complex nature by providing the fullest range of what is great and noble in human history. Whether arguing with his customary enthusiasm that "Books govern the world better than kings or priests" (xvii 321) or more philosophically that tragedy "is the refiner of the species; a discipline of humanity" (iv 200), his stance is clear and firm. Education liberates man from his primitive barbarism, from his intense preoccupation with his own narrow views and prejudices, and literature is the key to any such education. "The habitual study of poetry and works of imagination is one chief part of a well-grounded education. A taste for liberal art is necessary to complete the character of a gentleman. Science alone is hard and mechanical. It exercises the understanding upon things out of ourselves, while it leaves the affections unemployed, or engrossed with our own immediate, narrow interests" (iv 200).

To the new task of proclaiming the autonomy and power of literature Hazlitt summoned not only the artist himself but the critic. He also must liberate himself from older notions concerning his role as a servant of the preacher or the philosopher and establish himself as the proclaimer of the unique values of art and as the articulate and passionate spokesman of that distinctive emotional and imaginative encounter which is the core of the aesthetic experience itself. In short, he must possess something of that divine spark possessed by the artist himself.

THE LOGIC OF PASSION

As is so often the case, Hazlitt described his image of himself much better than his commentators. As he prefaces his observations on the Age of Elizabeth, he offers this apologia:

> If I can do any thing to rescue some of these writers from hopeless obscurity, and to do them right, without prejudice to well-deserved reputation, I shall have suceeded in what I chiefly propose. I shall not attempt, indeed, to adjust the spelling, or restore the pointing, as if the genius of poetry lay hid in errors of the press, but leaving these weightier matters of criticism to those who are more able and willing to bear the burden, try to bring out their real beauties to the eager sight, "draw the curtain of Time, and shew the picture of Genius," restraining my own admiration within reasonable bounds! [VI 176].

Surely Hazlitt, as these pages have revealed, is not a critic of uniform quality, of unvarying excellence. His work, particularly where enthusiasm runs ahead of thoughtful commentary, can be superficial, can be more concerned with the colorful metaphorical articulation of a response than with firm argument. It can be repetitious and consequently boring. It can neglect the many sides of a work of art in its intense preoccupation with some special effect or some particular facet. Yet at his best Hazlitt, the critic of finely tuned intuition and of strong feeling, brings to his criticism a genuine sense of the dominant thrust of a poem or a novel or a play, of its special quality which touches close to life and which prods the imagination and stirs the heart. When he is operating at the top of his power, one senses the master critic of English Romanticism at work, the critic who speaks for the new subjective values which become part of the early–nineteenth-century critical landscape. He, more than almost any other critic of his time, has that remarkable ability to draw us into the work of art, to enable us to feel its power, and to be better for the experience. His is the logic of passion.

NOTES

1. For a recent treatment embodying many of the ideas in this chapter, see my "No Better Reality: New Dimensions in Hazlitt's Aesthetics," in my *The English Romantics: Major Poetry and Critical Theory* (Lexington, Mass.: Heath, 1978), pp. 786–94.
2. *Hazlitt and the Spirit of the Age*, p. 1.
3. In *Criticism*, ed. Bate, pp. 340, 341.
4. In ibid., pp. 429, 430, 435, 432.
5. *The Letters of John Keats, 1814–1821*, ed. Hyder Edward Rollins, 2 vols. (Cambridge: Harvard University Press, 1958), I 192.

Bibliography

Abrams, M. H. *The Mirror and the Lamp: Romantic Theory and the Critical Tradition.* New York: Oxford University Press, 1953.
Albrecht, W. P. *Hazlitt and the Creative Imagination.* Lawrence: The University of Kansas Press, 1965.
———. "Hazlitt on the Poetry of Wit." *PMLA*, 75 (1960), 245–50.
———. "Hazlitt Studies, 1965–1972." *The Wordsworth Circle*, 6 (1975), 67–79.
———. "Hazlitt's Preference for Tragedy." *PMLA*, 71 (1956), 1042–51.
Baker, Herschel. *William Hazlitt.* Cambridge: The Belknap Press of Harvard University Press, 1962.
Bate, W. J. *The Burden of the Past and the English Poet.* Cambridge: The Belknap Press of Harvard University Press, 1970.
———. *From Classic to Romantic: Premises of Taste in Eighteenth-Century English Criticism.* Cambridge: Harvard University Press, 1946.
———. *John Keats.* Cambridge: The Belknap Press of Harvard University Press, 1963.
———. "The Sympathetic Imagination in Eighteenth-Century English Criticism." *ELH*, 12 (1945), 144–64.
Birrell, Augustine. *William Hazlitt.* English Men of Letters. London: Macmillan, 1926.
Bloom, Harold. *The Anxiety of Influence: A Theory of Poetry.* New York: Oxford University Press, 1973.
Bronson, B. H. "When Was Neoclassicism?" In *Studies in Criticism and Aesthetics, 1660–1800: Essays in Honor of Samuel Holt Monk.* Edd. Howard P. Anderson and John S. Shea. Minneapolis: The University of Minnesota Press, 1967. Pp. 13–35.
Bullitt, John M. "Hazlitt and the Romantic Conception of the Imagination." *Philological Quarterly*, 24, No. 4 (October 1945), 343–61.

Cain, Roy E. "David Hume and Adam Smith as Sources of the Concept of Sympathy in Hazlitt." *Papers on English Language and Literature*, 1, No. 2 (Spring 1965), 133–40.
Chase, Stanley P. "Hazlitt as a Critic of Art." *PMLA*, 39 (1924), 179–202.
Cragg, Gerald R. *Reason and Authority in the Eighteenth Century*. Cambridge: Cambridge University Press, 1964.
Criticism: The Major Texts. Ed. W. J. Bate. New York: Harcourt, Brace, 1952.
Dobrée, Bonamy. "William Hazlitt, 1778–1830." *A Review of English Literature*, 2, No. 1 (January 1961), 30–37.
Donohue, Joseph W., Jr. "Hazlitt's Sense of the Dramatic: Actor as Tragic Character." *Studies in English Literature, 1500–1900*, 5, No. 4 (Autumn 1965), 705–21.
Elliott, Eugene Clinton. "Reynolds and Hazlitt." *The Journal of Aesthetics and Art Criticism*, 21, No. 1 (Fall 1962), 73–79.
Garrod, H. W. "The Place of Hazlitt in English Criticism." In *The Profession of Poetry and Other Lectures*. Oxford: Clarendon, 1929. Pp. 92–109.
Gates, Payson G. "Bacon, Keats, and Hazlitt." *South Atlantic Quarterly*, 46 (1947), 239–51.
Gay, Peter. *The Enlightenment: An Interpretation*. New York: Knopf, 1967.
Hazlitt, William. *The Complete Works of William Hazlitt*. Ed. P. P. Howe. 21 vols. London: Dent, 1930–1934.
———. *Essays by William Hazlitt*. Ed. Percy Van Dyke Shelly. New York & Chicago: Scribner's, 1924.
———. *The Letters of William Hazlitt*. Edd. Herschel Moreland Sikes, Willard Hallam Bonner, and Gerald Lahey. New York: New York University Press, 1978.
———. *Literary Remains of the Late William Hazlitt with a Notice of His Life By His Son and Thoughts on His Genius and Writings*. Edd. E. L. Bulwer and Sergeant Talfourd. 2 vols. London: Saunders & Otley, 1836.
Howe, P. P. *The Life of William Hazlitt*. London: Secker [1922].

Ireland, Alexander. *William Hazlitt: Essayist and Critic*. London & New York: Warne, 1889.
Johnson, James William. *The Formation of English Neo-Classical Thought*. Princeton: Princeton University Press, 1967.
Keats, John. *The Letters of John Keats, 1814–1821*. Ed. Hyder Edward Rollins. 2 vols. Cambridge: Harvard University Press, 1958.
Kinnaird, John. *William Hazlitt: Critic of Power*. New York: Columbia University Press, 1978.
Lamb and Hazlitt: Further Letters and Records Hitherto Unpublished. Ed. William Carew Hazlitt. New York: Dodd, Mead, 1899.
Literary Criticism in England, 1660–1800. Ed. Gerald W. Chapman. New York: Knopf, 1966.
Maclean, Catherine M. *Born Under Saturn: A Biography of William Hazlitt*. London: Macmillan, 1943.
Mahoney, John L. "The Futuristic Imagination: Hazlitt's Approach to *Romeo and Juliet*." *The British Journal of Aesthetics*, 14 (1974), 65–67.
——. "Imitation and the Quest for Objectivity in English Romantic Theory." In *Proceedings of the Fourth Congress of the International Comparative Literature Association*. Ed. François Jost. The Hague: Mouton, 1966.
——. "In the Walks of Real Life: Hazlitt on the Restoration and Eighteenth Century." *Modern Language Studies*, 5 (1975), 21–30.
——. "No Better Reality: New Dimensions in Hazlitt's Aesthetics." In *The English Romantics: Major Poetry and Critical Theory*. Lexington, Mass.: Heath, 1978. Pp. 786–94.
O'Hara, J. D. "Hazlitt and the Functions of the Imagination." *PMLA*, 81 (1956), 552–62.
——. "Hazlitt and Romantic Criticism of the Fine Arts." *The Journal of Aesthetics and Art Criticism*, 27, No. 1 (Fall 1968), 73–85.
Park, Roy. *Hazlitt and the Spirit of the Age: Abstraction and Critical Theory*. Oxford: Clarendon, 1971.
Patterson, Charles I. "William Hazlitt as a Critic of Prose Fiction." *PMLA*, 68 (1953), 1001–16.
Pearson, Hesketh. *The Fool of Love*. London: Hamilton, 1934.

Perkins, David. *English Romantic Writers*. New York: Harcourt, Brace, World, 1967.
Reynolds, Sir Joshua. *Discourses*. Ed. Helen Zimmern. London: Scott, 1887.
Saintsbury, George. "Hazlitt." In *Essays in English Literature*. London: Rivington, Percival, 1890. Pp. 135–69.
Sallé, J.-C. "Hazlitt the Associationist." *Review of English Studies*, N.S. 15 (1964), 38–51.
Schneider, Elizabeth. *The Aesthetics of William Hazlitt: A Study of the Philosophical Basis of His Criticism*. Philadelphia: University of Pennsylvania Press, 1933.
Stephen, Sir Leslie. "William Hazlitt." In *Hours in a Library*. 4 vols. New York & London: Putnam, 1904. Repr. Grosse Pointe, Mich.: Scholarly Press, 1968. II 235–86.
Stephenson, H. W. *William Hazlitt and Hackney College*. London: Lindsey, 1930.
Sutherland, James. *A Preface to Eighteenth Century Poetry*. Oxford: Clarendon, 1948.
Thorpe, Clarence D. "Keats and Hazlitt: A Record of Personal Relationship and Critical Estimate." *PMLA*, 62 (1947), 487–502.
Trawick, Leonard Moses III. "Eighteenth Century Influences on the Criticism of William Hazlitt." Ph.D. Diss. Harvard University, 1961.
Tuveson, Ernest Lee. *The Imagination as a Means of Grace: Locke and the Aesthetics of Romanticism*. Berkeley & Los Angeles: University of California Press, 1960.
Wardle, Ralph M. *Hazlitt*. Lincoln: University of Nebraska Press, 1971.
Watson, George. *The Literary Critics: A Study of English Descriptive Criticism*. Harmondsworth & Baltimore: Penguin, 1962.
Wellek, René. *A History of Modern Criticism, 1750–1950*. II. *The Romantic Age*. New Haven: Yale University Press, 1955.
Whitehead, Alfred North. *Science and the Modern World*. New York: Macmillan, 1925.
Whitley, Alvin. "Hazlitt and the Theater." *The University of Texas Studies in English*, 34 (1955), 67–100.
Willey, Basil. *The Eighteenth Century Background: Studies in the Thought of the Period*. London: Chatto & Windus, 1940.

Youngren, William H. "Conceptualism and Neoclassic Generality." *ELH*, 47 (1980), 705–40.
———. "Generality in Augustan Satire." In *In Defense of Reading: A Reader's Approach to Literary Criticism*. Edd. Reuben A. Brower and Richard Poirier. New York: Dutton, 1962. Pp. 206–34.
———. "Generality, Science and Poetic Language in the Restoration." *ELH*, 35 (1968), 158–87.
Zeitlin, Jacob. *Hazlitt on English Literature: An Introduction to the Appreciation of Literature*. New York: Oxford University Press, 1913.

Index

Abrams, M. H., 18
Addison, Joseph, 22, 66
Akenside, Mark, 22, 23
Albrecht, W. P., 3, 4, 27, 31, 88
Anglo-Scottish literary theory, 21, 27–28, 33, 40, 75, 88, 91, 94
Anne, Queen, 50
Ariosto, 99
Aristotle, 11, 102
Association, Psychology of, 35, 88; Hazlitt on the working of, 91–92
Augustus Caesar, 10

Bacon, Francis, 10, 30, 31, 104
Baker, Herschel, 1, 2, 27, 51–52
Bate, Walter Jackson, 2, 3, 8, 17, 22, 27, 62–63, 99
Beaumont, Francis, 68
Bible, The, 47, 106
Birrell, Augustine, 1
Blake, William, 14, 23
Bloom, Harold, 99
Boccaccio, 99
Bonner, Willard Hallam, 3
Boyle, Robert, 11
British empirical tradition, 8, 27, 30, 40, 88
Bronson, B. H., 8–9, 21
Bullitt, John, 2
Bulwer, E. L., 1

Burke, Edmund, 22, 70, 90
Burnet, Thomas, 14
Burton, Robert, 39
Byron, George Gordon, Lord, 80–81

Cervantes, Miguel de, 57, 67, 90, 99
Chapman, George, 47
Charles I, 50
Charles II, 10, 50
Chase, Stanley, 3
Chatterton, Thomas, 23
Chaucer, Geoffrey, 16, 18; Hazlitt on, 48–50, 54–56, 82–83, 90, 93–94, 99
Coalescence, Psychology of, 35, 88, 91
Coleridge, Samuel Taylor, 62; Hazlitt on, 34, 52, 57, 79, 81
Collier, Jeremy, 109
Collins, William, 23
Condillac, Etienne Bonnot de, 74
Congreve, William, 48
Correggio, 70, 99
Cowley, Abraham, 90–91
Cragg, Gerald, 12, 14
Crashaw, Richard, 49

Dante Alighieri, 99

Darwin, Erasmus, 20
Davenant, William, 15
Davies, John, 49
Defoe, Daniel, 90
Dekker, Thomas, 47
Descartes, René, 10, 12
Dissenters, 28; *see also* Nonconformity
Donne, John, 49
Dryden, John, 10, 16–20, 47, 50, 66, 83, 98
Duff, William, 22

Fancy, Mental power of, 50
Farquhar, George, 48
Fielding, Henry, 57–58, 90, 97
Fletcher, John, 47, 68
French Revolution, The, 109

Garrod, H. W., 1
Gay, Peter, 10–11
Generality, 19, 51
Genius, 33, 34; Hazlitt on, 40, 97–99
Gerard, Alexander, 22
Godwin, William, 29, 84
Goldsmith, Oliver, 20
Gray, Thomas, 23
Guido Reni, 100
Gusto, Hazlitt's general discussions of, 61–64, 75; on Milton's, 68–69; in Chaucer and Spenser, 69–70; in Shakespeare's plays, 67–68; in painting, 70–71; in tragedy, 64–67

Hackney, 29
Hartley, David, 30, 31, 92
Hazlitt, William Carew (grandson) 36n8

Hazlitt, William: eighteenth-century backgrounds of his criticism, 9–25; his Nonconformist roots, 28–30; education and philosophical influences at Unitarian New College, Hackney, 30–32; further philosophical influences, 33–35; his response to earlier critics, desire to be a new kind of critic, 37–43

Works and subjects of his criticism: "On Abstract Ideas," 50; *Characteristics*, 73; *Essay on the Principles of Human Action*, 74, 84; "On Genius and Common Sense," 41, 64; "On Genius and Originality," 98; "On Poetry in General," 63–64, 87, 101; *Prospectus for a History of English Philosophy*, 27; "On Reason and Imagination," 52; *A View of the English Stage*, 38; on his contemporaries, 42–43, 57, 99; on Dryden and Restoration tragedians, 47; on Elizabethan writers, 42, 97, 112; on fiction, 57–58; on Old English literature, 42; as painter–critic, 52; on Restoration comedy, 48; on seventeenth-century dramatists in England, France, Germany, 47; on tragedy, 64–67; on Wordsworth and Rousseau and the problem of egotism, 78–80.

Helvétius, Claude Adrien, 31, 74
Heywood, Thomas, 47
Hobbes, Thomas, 8, 16, 17, 22, 27, 30, 31, 34, 59, 74, 84, 92
Hogarth, William, 46, 54, 77
Homer, 16, 18, 84, 99, 106

INDEX

Horace, 17
Howe, P. P., 1
Hume, David, 30, 34
Hutcheson, Francis, 8, 22, 33, 34, 75

Imagination, Faculty of, 2, 5, 17, 18, 23, 33, 34; Hazlitt on, 85–89
Ireland, Alexander, 1

Johnson, James, 16–17
Johnson, Samuel, 16–20, 39, 50, 51, 70, 79, 98
Jonson, Ben, 16, 18, 47, 56–57
Judgment, Faculty of, 16, 17, 98; *see also* Reason

Kames, Henry Home, Lord, 22, 34
Kant, Immanuel, 34, 59
Keats, John, 91–92, 97, 108
Kinnaird, John, 3, 27

Lahey, Gerald, 3
Lake school of poetry, 79
Lamb, Charles, 7, 54
Landor, Walter Savage, 84
Le Sage, Alain René, 58
Lillo, George, 66
Locke, John, 8, 13, 22, 27, 30–31, 51, 59
Lorrain, Claude, 71
Lyrical Ballads, Preface to the Second Edition of (1800), 102, 103, 110

Maclean, Catherine, 1
Macpherson, James, 23; his *Ossian*, 106
Marlowe, Christopher, 47, 68

Marston, John, 47
Metaphysical poets and poetry, 18, 20, 49, 93
Michelangelo, 71, 79
Middleton, Thomas, 47
Milton, John, Hazlitt on, 48–50; disinterestedness in *Paradise Lost, Paradise Regained, Samson Agonistes*, 82–84, 90; on *Lycidas*, 89–90, 99–100; on his genius, 108–109
Molière, 67
Moore, Edward, 65–66

Nature, Neoclassic views of, 9–20, 98, 109; Hazlitt on, 45–46, 51–52
Newton, Isaac, 11
Nonconformity, 1, 27–29; *see also* Dissenters

O'Hara, J. D., 3, 4, 27
Otway, Thomas, 66

Paine, Thomas, 29
Park, Roy, 3, 27, 32, 43, 52, 102
Patterson, Charles, 3–4
Pearson, Hesketh, 1
Percy, Thomas, 23
Plato, 59, 102
Pope, Alexander, 11–21; Hazlitt on, 50, 51, 79, 83–84, 98, 100
Price, Richard, 28
Priestley, Joseph, 28
Progress and decline in the arts, Hazlitt on, 50, 99–100

Rabelais, François, 67
Raphael, 70, 99
Ray, John, 11

Reason, Faculty of, 13–15, 17, 23, 88, 92, 98; *see also* Judgment
Reformation, The, 47
Reid, Thomas, 34
Rembrandt, 70
Reynolds, Sir Joshua, 32, 40, 51, 59, 98
Richardson, Samuel, 58, 90
Rousseau, Jean-Jacques, 27, 33, 77–78
Royal Society, 11
Rubens, Peter Paul, 70
Rymer, Thomas, 15

Saintsbury, George, 1
Sallé, J.-C., 3
Schlegel, A. W., 56
Schneider, Elizabeth, 2, 7, 27, 30, 33, 74, 75
Scott, Sir Walter, 80, 81, 91
Sentiment, Hazlitt on, 90
Shaftesbury, Anthony Ashley Cooper, third Earl of, 8, 22, 33, 75, 76
Shakespeare, William, 16, 18; Hazlitt on his tragedy in general, 47; on his view and treatment of nature, 48–50, 58–59; on his treatment of character, with specific references to *King Lear*, *Macbeth*, *Othello*, *Richard III*, *Henry IV, Part I*, 53–56; on his comedy, e.g., *Much Ado About Nothing*, *Henry IV, Part I*, 55–56; his sympathetic imagination in *Antony and Cleopatra*, *Hamlet*, *Henry IV, Part I*, *Macbeth*, *Othello*, *Romeo and Juliet*, *The Tempest*, and his lack of it in *Measure for Measure*, 95–97; on the moral dimension of his plays, e.g., *Coriolanus*, *Henry IV, Part II*, *King Lear*, 59, 107–108
Shelley, Percy Bysshe, 57, 102–103, 111
Shelly, Percy Van Dyke, 1
Sheridan, Richard Brinsley, 109
Sidney, Philip, 15
Sikes, Herschel Moreland, 3
Smith, Adam, 22, 34
Smollett, Tobias, 58, 90
Sophocles, 47
Spenser, Edmund, 48–50, 69–70, 91, 93, 99
Steele, Richard, 109
Sprat, Thomas, 11
Stephen, Sir Leslie, 1, 28–29
Stephenson, H. W., 29
Stewart, Dugald, 34
Sutherland, James, 19, 21
Swift, Jonathan, 19, 51
Sympathy, 2, 33, 34; Hazlitt on, 74–75, 84–85, 87, 94

Tasso, 100
Taste, 33, 35, 40, 41
Thompson, James, 23, 84
Tuileries, 92–93
Titian, 70, 99
Trawick, Leonard, 27
Tucker, Abraham, 34

Unitarian New College, Hackney, 29

Vanbrugh, John, 48
Van Dyke, Anthony, 70, 100
Vergil, 16, 18

Walker, Sarah, 1

INDEX

Walpole, Horace, 23
Warton, Joseph, 21, 23, 50
Warton, Thomas, 23
Webster, John, 47
Wellek, René, 7, 74
West, Benjamin, 71
Whitehead, Alfred North, 45–46
Whitley, Alvin, 4
Wit, 2, 16, 17; Hazlitt on, 50
Wordsworth, William, 40, 45, 74, 102, 103, 110; Hazlitt on his egotism, 75–79; on his lack of objectivity in *The Excursion*, 79, 90; dissatisfied with the Platonic argument of the *Immortality Ode*, 95
Wycherley, William, 48

Young, Edward, 23, 90

www.ingramcontent.com/pod-product-compliance
Lightning Source LLC
Chambersburg PA
CBHW020656300426
44112CB00007B/405